5 Ingredient Favorites

RACHEL LANE

5 Ingredient Favorites

OVER **140** DELICIOUS RECIPES

THE READER'S DIGEST ASSOCIATION, INC.
NEW YORK, NEW YORK / MONTREAL / SYDNEY / SINGAPORE

A READER'S DIGEST BOOK

This edition published by
The Reader's Digest Association, Inc.,
by arrangement with McRae Books Srl

5 Ingredient Favorites was created and produced by
McRae Publishing Ltd, London
info@mcraebooks.com

FOR MCRAE BOOKS
Project Director: Anne McRae
Art Director: Marco Nardi
Photography: Brent Parker Jones
Photographic Art Direction: Neil Hargreaves
Texts: Rachel Lane
Food Styling: Lee Blaycock, Neil Hargreaves
Layouts: Aurora Granata
Prepress: Filippo Delle Monache, Davide Gasparri

FOR READER'S DIGEST
U.S. Project Editor: Andrea Chesman
Canadian Project Editor: Pamela Chichinskas
Australian Project Editor: Annette Carter
Copy Editor: Emily Bigelow
Senior Art Director: George McKeon
Executive Editor, Trade Publishing: Dolores York
Associate Publisher, Trade Publishing: Rosanne McManus
President and Publisher, Trade Publishing: Harold Clarke

ISBN 978-1-60652-247-9

We are committed to both the quality of our products and
the service we provide to our customers. We value your
comments, so please feel free to contact us.

The Reader's Digest Association, Inc.
Adult Trade Publishing
44 S. Broadway
White Plains, NY 10601

NOTE TO OUR READERS
Eating eggs or egg whites that are not completely cooked
poses the possibility of salmonella food poisoning. The risk
is greater for pregnant women, the elderly, the very young,
and persons with impaired immune systems. If you are
concerned about salmonella, you can use reconstituted
powdered egg whites or pasteurized eggs.

For more Reader's Digest products and information, visit
our website:
    www.rd.com (in the United States)
    www.readersdigest.ca (in Canada)
    www.readersdigest.com.au (in Australia)
    www.readersdigest.com.nz (in New Zealand)

Printed in China

5 7 9 10 8 6 4

The level of difficulty for each recipe is given on a scale from
1 (easy) to 3 (complicated).

CONTENTS

INTRODUCTION

Cooking with just a handful of ingredients will not only save you time and money but will also let you rediscover the natural, basic flavors of foods. You will learn how to combine them so that they subtly complement each other without creating an overload of contradictory tastes and aromas. By using a contained ingredient palette, these recipes concentrate on classic taste combinations, such as pasta, noodles, or rice with tomatoes and fresh herbs, or grilled fish or meat served with a starchy vegetable. Each is bathed in a simple sauce or dusted with spices. We've identified the level of difficulty for each recipe (1=easy to 3= complicated) to take the work out of meal planning. While almost all of these dishes are simple to prepare, you'll find some intriguing and challenging recipes, too, like the Avocado Sushi Rolls on page 24 and the Stuffed Mini Pumpkins on page 156.

This book delivers on the promise of its title: Each recipe has five ingredients—with salt and water as extras in just a few. The amount of salt in a recipe is a very personal choice; some people have almost entirely eliminated it from their diets for health reasons, while others give their food a few liberal shakes. So it is a good idea to adjust the salt in these recipes to suit your personal taste. Water is a tricky ingredient to count. You can't cook pasta without water but at the end of the cooking process it gets tossed out; for simplicity's sake, it is not counted as an ingredient at all.

In chapter eight, which features pork, lamb, and beef, be sure to follow your own inclinations for cooking times. For some people, a beef steak that isn't dripping blood is overcooked, while others prefer a blackened surface without a trace of pink inside. However, keep in mind that for health reasons pork absolutely needs to be heated all the way through to at least 160°F (71°C). You may want to invest in a meat thermometer to be sure it is always safely done.

The book is divided into nine easy-to-consult chapters. You'll find dishes for every occasion—from afterschool snacks and light-lunch soups and salads to heartier offerings featuring pasta, noodles, and grains. And if you need crowd-pleasing recipes for family meals or entertaining, there are chapters filled with dishes based on versatile and protein-packed seafood, chicken and meat. The finale is a chapter of memorable, mouthwatering desserts.

All 141 recipes have been tested and illustrated by a striking photograph, which will help even novice cooks to prepare and present these simple, gourmet dishes with ease and flair. You'll be surprised by the sheer variety of good food that can be prepared with a minimum of ingredients—and fuss!

SNACKS, STARTERS AND LUNCHES

BLUEBERRY SMOOTHIE

Purée the blueberries in a food processor or blender. • Add the milk, yogurt, honey, and ice. Blend until smooth and thick. • Pour into two large glasses. • Serve.

16

3$\frac{1}{2}$ cups (500 g) fresh blueberries

1 cup (250 ml) milk

$\frac{1}{2}$ cup (125 ml) thick, Greek-style yogurt

2 teaspoons (10 ml) honey

10 ice cubes, crushed

Serves: 2
Preparation: 10 minutes
Level: 1

CHOCOLATE AND BANANA SMOOTHIE

Cut the bananas into pieces and put in a food processor or blender. • Add the milk, yogurt, chocolate syrup, and ice. Blend until smooth and thick. • Pour the smoothie into two large glasses.
• Serve at once.

2   **large ripe bananas**

1   **cup (250 ml) milk**

1/2 **cup (125 ml) vanilla yogurt**

1/4 **cup (60 ml) chocolate syrup or topping**

10 **ice cubes, crushed**

Serves: 2
Preparation: 10 minutes
Level: 1

■ ■ ■ *Use your favorite store-bought chocolate syrup or ice cream topping to make this smoothie. Most come in plastic bottles with nozzles. Squeeze extra syrup around the sides of the empty glasses to add flavor and to make your smoothie look even more enticing.*

GOAT CHEESE AND MINT TARTS

Line four small tart pans with the short-crust pastry. Refrigerate for 10 minutes. • Preheat the oven to 300°F (150°C/gas 2). • Remove the pastry from the refrigerator. Cover each pastry shell with a square of waxed paper and fill with 1 tablespoon of uncooked rice. • Place in the oven and bake blind for about 10 minutes, until pastry has just begun to color. • Turn the oven temperature up to 350°F (180°C/gas 4). • Whisk the eggs in a medium bowl. • Add the chopped goat cheese and mint and stir well to combine. • Fill the tart shells with this filling. Season to taste with cracked pepper. • Bake for about 10 minutes, until the filling turns golden. • Serve warm or at room temperature, garnished with the mint leaves.

2 sheets frozen short-crust pie pastry, thawed
3 large eggs
8 ounces (250 g) soft goat cheese, crumbled
3 tablespoons coarsely chopped fresh mint leaves + whole leaves to garnish
   Cracked pepper

Serves: 4
Preparation: 15 minutes + 10 minutes to chill
Cooking: 20 minutes
Level: 1

CHEESE AND SWEET POTATO PASTIES

22

Preheat the oven to 425°F (220°C/gas 7). Line a large baking sheet with parchment paper. • Dice the sweet potatoes into 1/2-inch (1-cm) cubes. • Place in a steamer over a saucepan of boiling water. Steam until soft, about 5 minutes.

• Combine the sweet potatoes, ricotta, Parmesan, and pesto in a medium bowl.

• Lay the pastry sheets on a clean work surface and cut out four large circles.

• Divide the sweet potato mixture into four equal portions. Place in the center of each pastry circle. • Fold the pastry over the filling to make a half-moon shape. Pinch the edges together and seal with a little water. • Place the pasties on the prepared baking sheet and lightly brush the tops with water. • Bake for about 25 minutes, until pale golden brown. • Serve hot.

2 medium sweet potatoes, peeled

3/4 cup (180 g) ricotta cheese, drained

1/4 cup (30 g) freshly grated Parmesan cheese

2 tablespoons basil pesto

2 sheets frozen puff pastry, thawed

Serves: 4
Preparation: 20 minutes
Cooking: 30 minutes
Level: 1

AVOCADO SUSHI ROLLS

Wash the rice in a colander under cold running water, tossing gently until the water runs clear. • Combine the rice and 3 cups (750 ml) water in a medium saucepan. • Bring to a boil over low heat and simmer for 5 minutes. • Remove from the heat, cover, and leave for 15 minutes. • Place the rice in a large bowl and gradually stir in the vinegar until well combined. Allow to cool a little. • Lay a sheet of nori, shiny side down, on a bamboo mat. • Spread with one-fifth of the rice, leaving a $3/4$-inch (2-cm) border at one end. • Slice the avocado into strips lengthwise. • Make a line of avocado across the rice, $1^{1}/2$ inches (4 cm) in from the edge without the border. • Roll the mat over to enclose the avocado and continue rolling to form a firm roll. Use a little water to seal the seam. • Repeat this same process with the remaining nori sheets. • Trim the ends and cut each roll into six slices. Serve with the soy sauce for dipping.

$2^{1}/2$ cups (500 g) short-grain white rice

5 nori sheets

$1/4$ cup (60 ml) rice wine vinegar

1 avocado, halved and pitted (stoned)

$1/2$ cup (125 ml) soy sauce

Serves: 4
Preparation: 35 minutes
Cooking: 20 minutes
Level: 2

EGGPLANT DIP WITH TOASTED PITA

Preheat the oven to 400°F (200°C/ gas 6). • Place the eggplant on a baking sheet and pierce in few places with a fork. • Bake for about 1 hour, until softened. • Allow the eggplant to cool a little. Remove and discard the skin and coarsely chop the flesh. • Place the flesh in a sieve and squeeze out any excess liquid. • Using a fork, mash eggplant in a medium-sized bowl. • Add the oil, lemon juice, and garlic. Stir well to combine. • Place in a serving bowl. • Serve with toasted pita bread.

1   medium (about 1 pound/500 g) eggplant (aubergine)

3   tablespoons (45 ml) extra-virgin olive oil

2   tablespoons (30 ml) freshly squeezed lemon juice

2   cloves garlic, finely chopped

4   pita breads, sliced into wedges and toasted

Serves: 2–4
Preparation: 10 minutes
Cooking: 1 hour
Level: 1

CARAMELIZED ONION AND SPINACH TARTS

Combine the onions and oil in a heavy saucepan over low heat and simmer, stirring often, until caramelized, about 30 minutes. • Line four small fluted tart pans with short-crust pastry. Refrigerate for 10 minutes. • Preheat the oven to 300°F (150°C/gas 2). • Remove the pastry from the refrigerator. Cover each pastry shell with a square of waxed paper and fill with 1 tablespoon of rice. Place in the oven and blind bake for about 10 minutes, until the pastry has just begun to color. • Turn the oven temperature up to 350°F (180°C/gas 4). • Combine the onions, spinach, and salt in a medium bowl. • Fill the tart shells with spinach and onion filling. • Bake for 10 more minutes, or until the pastry is pale golden brown. • Serve hot or at room temperature.

4	large yellow onions, sliced
2	tablespoons extra-virgin olive oil
2	sheets frozen short-crust pie pastry, thawed
4	large handfuls baby spinach leaves
1/2	teaspoon salt

Serves: 4
Preparation: 15 minutes
 + 10 minutes to chill
Cooking: 50 minutes
Level: 1

AVOCADO AND BACON BURRITO

Fry the bacon in a large frying pan over medium-high heat until crisp, about 6 minutes. • Slice the avocado halves lengthwise into 4–6 pieces. • Heat the tortillas in a frying pan one at a time until they begin to color. • Lay the tortillas on a clean work surface and spread with the salsa. • Evenly divide the avocado, bacon, and spinach among the tortillas. • Fold to enclose the filling. • Serve hot.

8   slices bacon, rind removed, if necessary
2   avocados, halved and pitted (stoned)
1½ cups baby spinach leaves
4   flour tortillas
⅓   cup (90 ml) salsa or fruit chutney

Serves: 4
Preparation: 5 minutes
Cooking: 10 minutes
Level: 1

GUACAMOLE WITH CORN CHIPS

Dice the avocado. Place in a medium bowl and use a fork to roughly mash.
• Add the onion, olives, and lemon juice. Stir well to combine. • Transfer the guacamole to a small serving bowl. Serve with the corn chips.

2 avocados, halved and pitted (stoned)

1 small red onion, finely diced

¼ cup (50 g) pitted black olives, diced

3 tablespoons (45 ml) freshly squeezed lemon juice

Corn chips, to serve

Serves: 2
Preparation: 10 minutes
Level: 1

SAUSAGE ROLLS

Preheat the oven to 425°F (220°C/gas 7). Line a large baking sheet with parchment paper. • Combine the sausage meat, onion, thyme, and 1/3 cup (90 g) of the chutney in a medium bowl. • Lay the pastry sheets out on a clean work surface and cut in half lengthwise.

• Place the sausage mixture in a piping bag with a large plain tip. • Pipe a line of mixture down the center of each pastry sheet. Add additional mixture if necessary until all is used. • Roll the pastry around the sausage meat and seal the edges. Brush the tops with a little water. • Cut each log in half and prick the tops with a fork. • Place the sausage rolls seam-side down on the prepared baking sheet. • Bake for 15–20 minutes, until golden brown. • Serve hot with the remaining chutney.

2   sheets puff pastry
1   pound (500 g) sausage meat
1   onion, finely diced
2   tablespoons finely chopped fresh thyme
1   cup (250 g) fruit chutney

Serves: 4
Preparation: 15 minutes
Cooking: 15–20 minutes
Level: 1

CHICKEN RICE PAPER ROLLS

Place the noodles in a medium bowl and soak in hot water until soft, about 5 minutes. • Drain, roughly chop into shorter lengths, and return to the bowl. • Add the chicken, mint, and 1 tablespoon of chili sauce and combine well. • Soak the rice paper wrappers one at a time in a large bowl of warm water until they soften, about 2 minutes. • Lay the softened sheets on a clean work surface. • Place about 1 tablespoon of the filling mixture along the bottom third of the wrapper, allowing enough space at the sides to fold over. • Fold the sides inward and firmly roll up the wrapper. • Repeat this process with the remaining wrappers. • Place the rolls, seam side down, on a serving plate. • Serve with remaining chili sauce for dipping.

■■■ *If not serving immediately, cover the rice paper rolls with a clean damp kitchen towel to prevent them from drying out.*

3 ounces (90 g) vermicelli rice noodles

16 rice paper wrappers

1 chicken breast, grilled and shredded

3 tablespoons finely chopped fresh Vietnamese (or other) mint

½ cup (125 ml) Thai sweet chili sauce

Serves: 4
Preparation: 40 minutes
Level: 1

CORN FRITTERS

38

Whisk the egg and corn liquid together in a medium bowl. • Add the corn and flour and stir with a fork until just combined. • Heat the oil in a large frying pan over medium-high heat. • Drop tablespoons of batter into the oil and cook until golden brown, about 3 minutes on each side. • Place the fritters on paper towels to drain off any excess oil. • Serve hot with the chutney for dipping.

1   large egg
1   (14-ounce/400-g) can corn (sweet corn) kernels, drained + ¼ cup (60 ml) of the liquid reserved
1   cup (150 g) self-rising flour
¼   cup (60 ml) extra-virgin olive oil
½   cup (125 g) fruit chutney

Serves: 4
Preparation: 15 minutes
Cooking: 15 minutes
Level: 1

TOMATO AND FETA CHEESE BRUSCHETTA

Place the tomatoes on a small baking sheet and drizzle with 1 tablespoon of the reserved feta oil. • Place under a hot broiler (grill) and cook until the tomatoes begin to collapse, 3–4 minutes. • Lightly brush the sourdough bread with the remaining oil and broil (grill) until golden. • Combine the tomatoes, feta, and tarragon in a medium bowl. Add cracked pepper to taste. • Arrange the mixture on top of the toasted bread. • Broil for 2 more minutes. Serve hot.

12   red cherry tomatoes
½   cup (120 g) marinated feta, crumbled, with 3 tablespoons (45 ml) of the oil reserved
2   thick slices sourdough bread
½   tablespoon roughly chopped fresh tarragon
     Cracked pepper

Serves: 1–2
Preparation: 5 minutes
Cooking: 10 minutes
Level: 1

■ ■ ■ *If preferred, use extra-virgin olive oil and plain feta instead of marinated feta.*

SALMON CAKES WITH CILANTRO

42

Finely dice the salmon and transfer to a medium bowl. • Add the egg whites and cilantro and stir to combine well. • Heat the oil in a large frying pan over medium-high heat. • Place 2 tablespoons of the salmon mixture in the oil and fry until light golden, about 1 minute on each side. • Repeat with the remaining salmon mixture. • Place the salmon cakes on paper towels to drain off any excess oil. • Serve hot with chili sauce for dipping.

1   pound (500 g) salmon fillet, skin and bones removed

2   egg whites, lightly beaten

3   tablespoons finely chopped fresh cilantro (coriander)

1   cup (250 ml) canola oil

½   cup (125 ml) Thai sweet chili sauce

Serves: 4
Preparation: 10 minutes
Cooking: 5 minutes
Level: 1

POLENTA CHIPS WITH TOMATO SALSA

Line a 7 x 11-inch (18 x 28-cm) baking pan with waxed paper. • Bring the stock to a boil in a large saucepan. • Add the polenta, reduce the heat to low, and cook, stirring often, for 30 minutes, or until the polenta begins to come away from the sides of the pan. • Stir in the Parmesan. • Pour the polenta into the prepared baking dish and spread evenly. • Cover and refrigerate until firm, about 1 hour. • Cut the polenta into 12 rectangles. • Heat the oil in a large frying pan. • Fry the polenta until light brown and crisp on all sides. • Place on paper towels to drain off any excess oil. • Serve hot with the tomato salsa.

8 **cups (2 liters) vegetable stock**

2 **cups (400 g) polenta**

3/4 **cup (120 g) freshly grated Parmesan cheese**

1 **cup (250 ml) extra-virgin olive oil**

1 **cup (250 ml) tomato salsa**

Serves: 4
Preparation: 15 minutes + 1 hour to firm the polenta
Cooking: 40 minutes
Level: 2

DUCK AND SNOW PEA WRAPS

Place the duck in a small frying pan over medium heat, skin side down. Cook until browned and cooked through, 8–10 minutes on each side. • Remove the fat and thinly slice the meat. • Heat the tortillas one at a time in a frying pan over medium until they begin to color. • Lay the hot tortillas on a clean work surface and spread with the hoisin sauce. • Evenly divide the duck, snow peas, and cucumber among the tortillas. • Fold to enclose the filling. Serve hot.

1   **boneless duck breast**

2   **small flour tortillas**

¼   **cup (60 ml) hoisin sauce**

10   **snow peas (sugar peas/mangetout), trimmed and finely sliced lengthwise**

1   **small cucumber, finely sliced lengthwise**

Serves: 2
Preparation: 10 minutes
Cooking: 20 minutes
Level: 1

■ ■ ■ *Hoisin sauce, also known as Peking sauce, is a thick, sweet, and spicy mixture of soybeans, salt, garlic, chilies, and other spices. Buy it at an ethnic food store or in the Asian foods section of your local supermarket.*

CAJUN POTATO WEDGES

Preheat oven to 375°F (190°C/gas 5).
• Pour the oil into a large baking dish.
Place in the oven for 5 minutes, or until
hot. • Cut the potatoes into wedges and
roll in the Cajun spice mix. • Add the
potatoes to the hot oil and toss to coat
well. • Bake for 25–30 minutes, until
golden, turning occasionally. • Serve
hot with the sour cream and salsa
for dipping.

½ cup (125 ml)
   vegetable oil

4 medium potatoes,
   peeled

2 tablespoons Cajun
   spice mix

½ cup (125 ml) sour
   cream

½ cup (125 g) tomato
   salsa

Serves: 4
Preparation: 10 minutes
Cooking: 25–30 minutes
Level: 1

■ ■ ■ *Cajun spice mix is usually made with a mixture*
of salt, pepper, onion powder, garlic powder, cayenne,
and thyme. Substitute any highly flavored spice or
barbecue mix you have on hand.

SMOKED SALMON FILO PARCELS

Preheat the oven to 425°F (220°C/gas 7). Lightly butter a baking sheet. • Rinse the spinach under cold running water. Do not drain but place in a saucepan over medium-high heat with the water clinging to the leaves. Stir often and cook until the leaves are wilted and bright green, 3–5 minutes. • Let cool a little, then gently squeeze out the excess moisture. Chop coarsely with a large knife. • Combine the salmon, spinach, and crème fraîche in a medium bowl. • Place one sheet of pastry on a clean work surface. • Using a pastry brush, paint the sheet with melted butter and lay another sheet on top. Cut in half lengthwise. • Place a quarter of the salmon mixture at the top of a pastry sheet. • Fold the pastry over to form a triangular shape and continue folding down to the end. Seal and brush the top with a little melted butter. • Repeat this process with the remaining filling mixture and pastry. • Place the

2   cups baby spinach leaves

4   slices smoked salmon, chopped

½   cup (125 ml) crème fraîche or sour cream

4   sheets phyllo (filo) pastry

¼   cup (60 g) butter, melted

Serves: 2
Preparation: 25 minutes
Cooking: 30 minutes
Level: 1

parcels on the prepared baking sheet.
Bake for 20–25 minutes, until the pastry
is golden and crisp. • Serve hot or at
room temperature.

■■■ *Cover phyllo (filo) pastry with a clean damp
kitchen towel to prevent it from drying out.*

SOUPS

TOMATO AND TARRAGON SOUP

Preheat the oven to 350°F (180°C/gas 4). • Place the tomatoes on a baking sheet. Bake for about 20 minutes, until the tomatoes are soft and begin to collapse. Remove the skins and set aside. • Peel the onions and place on a separate baking sheet. Bake for about 25 minutes, until light golden in color. • Combine the tomatoes, onions, stock, and sugar in a medium saucepan. Bring to a boil and then reduce to a simmer. • Add the tarragon and simmer for 5 minutes. • Purée the soup with a hand-held blender or in a food processor. • Return to the heat for 2–3 minutes. Serve hot.

12 large tomatoes

4 medium yellow onions

3 cups (750 ml) vegetable stock

1½ teaspoons sugar

3 tablespoons finely chopped fresh tarragon

Serves: 4
Preparation: 10 minutes
Cooking: About 1 hour
Level: 1

■ ■ ■ *The baked onions give this soup a deliciously sweet flavor. If preferred, replace the tarragon with the same quantity of finely chopped basil.*

MINTY PEA SOUP

Chop the peas in a food processor until smooth. Put in a medium saucepan.
• Add the stock, mint, and crumbled goat cheese. • Bring to a boil over medium heat and simmer gently for 5 minutes.
• Ladle into bowls and garnish with the extra goat cheese and mint leaves. Serve hot.

2½ cups (400 g) frozen peas, thawed

4 cups (1 liter) vegetable stock

3 tablespoons finely sliced mint + extra leaves to garnish

3 ounces (90 g) goat cheese + extra to garnish

Serves: 4
Preparation: 10 minutes
Cooking: 10 minutes
Level: 1

GINGER CHICKEN SOUP

Combine the stock, chicken breasts, and ginger in a large saucepan. • Bring to a boil and simmer gently for 15 minutes. • Reduce the heat and remove the chicken breasts. • Add the carrot and soy sauce to the pan. • Shred the chicken and divide evenly among four serving bowls. Pour the soup over the top and serve hot.

60

5	cups (1.25 liters) chicken stock
2	small boneless, skinless chicken breasts
$1\frac{1}{2}$	tablespoons grated fresh ginger
2	large carrots, grated
2	tablespoons (30 ml) soy sauce

Serves: 4
Preparation: 10 minutes
Cooking: 20 minutes
Level: 1

SPICY SAUSAGE AND TOMATO SOUP

62

Combine the stock, tomatoes, sausage, and beans in a large saucepan. • Bring to a boil and simmer gently for 10 minutes. • Add the thyme and simmer for 5 more minutes. • Serve hot.

2 cups (500 ml) vegetable stock

2 (14-ounce/400-g) cans chopped tomatoes, with juice

8 ounces (250 g) Spanish chorizo sausage, peeled and sliced

1 (14-ounce/400-g) can cannellini beans, drained

2 tablespoons coarsely chopped fresh thyme

Serves: 4
Preparation: 10 minutes
Cooking: 15 minutes
Level: 1

■ ■ ■ *Chorizo is a spicy sausage made in Mexico or Spain. Spanish chorizo is made with smoked pork while Mexican chorizo is made with fresh pork. If preferred, replace the Spanish chorizo with another type of highly seasoned sausage.*

ROASTED BELL PEPPER SOUP

Preheat the oven to 400°F (200°C/gas 6). • Place the bell peppers on a baking sheet. • Roast until the skins begin to blister and blacken, about 30 minutes. • Remove the bell peppers from the oven and place in a small bowl. • Cover with plastic wrap (cling film) and allow to cool for 10 minutes. • Remove the seeds and skins from the bell peppers. • Slice into quarters. • Combine the bell peppers, chicken stock, onions, tomatoes, and garlic in a large saucepan. • Bring to a boil and simmer for 15 minutes. • Purée the soup with a hand-held blender or in a food processor. • Reheat the soup for 2–3 minutes, then serve hot.

5 medium red bell peppers (capsicums)

4 cups (1 liter) chicken stock

2 yellow onions, quartered

1 (14-ounce/400-g) can chopped tomatoes, with juice

2 cloves garlic, chopped

Serves: 4
Preparation: 30 minutes + 10 minutes to cool
Cooking: 50 minutes
Level: 2

SWEET POTATO SOUP

Combine the sweet potatoes and vegetable stock in a large saucepan over medium heat. Bring to a boil. • Simmer for 15 minutes, or until the potatoes are soft. • Purée with a hand-held blender or in a food processor. • Return to the heat and add the coconut milk, lime juice, and chilies. • Gently simmer for 5 more minutes. • Serve hot.

2   pounds (1 kg) sweet potatoes, peeled and coarsely chopped

3   cups (750 ml) vegetable stock

1   (14-ounce/400-ml) can coconut milk

1/4 cup (60 ml) freshly squeezed lime juice

2   small fresh red chiles, seeded and finely sliced

Serves: 4
Preparation: 15 minutes
Cooking: 20 minutes
Level: 1

CORN SOUP

Heat the butter in a large saucepan over medium heat. • Add the corn and onion and simmer for 5 minutes. • Add the chicken stock and bring to a boil. Simmer for 10 minutes, or until the corn is tender. • Add the cream and simmer gently for 5 more minutes. • Purée with a hand-held blender or in a food processor. • Reheat the soup for 2–3 minutes, then serve hot.

¹/₄ cup (60 g) butter

Kernels from 5 ears (cobs) corn (sweet corn)

2 large onions, sliced

4 cups (1 liter) chicken stock

¹/₂ cup (125 ml) light (single) cream

Serves: 4
Preparation: 10 minutes
Cooking: 20 minutes
Level: 1

CABBAGE AND POTATO SOUP

Heat the oil in a large saucepan over medium-low heat. Add the cabbage and sauté for 10 minutes. • Slice the potatoes thinly into wedges and add to the cabbage. • Add the chicken stock and bring to a boil. • Simmer until potatoes are tender, about 10 minutes. • Add the parsley and serve hot.

¼ **cup (60 ml) walnut oil**

¼ **Savoy cabbage (about 2 pounds/ 1 kg), cored and thinly shredded**

1 **pound (500 g) potatoes, scrubbed, with peel**

5 **cups (1.25 liters) chicken stock**

⅓ **cup coarsely chopped fresh parsley**

Serves: 4
Preparation: 10 minutes
Cooking: 25 minutes
Level: 1

■ ■ ■ *Walnut oil will add a delicious nutty flavor to this soup. You may replace it with the same amount of extra-virgin olive oil, if preferred.*

SQUASH AND PANCETTA SOUP

Place the pancetta in a large saucepan over medium heat and fry until crisp.
• Remove the pancetta and drain on paper towels. • Add the onion and garlic to the remaining oil in the saucepan and sauté for 3 minutes, or until just tender.
• Add the squash and stock and bring to the boil. • Simmer for 12 minutes, or until the squash is tender. • Purée with a hand-held blender or in a food processor. • Return to the heat, add the pancetta, and reheat for 2–3 minutes. Serve hot.

8   ounces (250 g) sliced pancetta, coarsely chopped
1   onion, finely chopped
3   cloves garlic, coarsely chopped
2   pounds (1 kg) butternut squash (pumpkin), peeled, seeded, and coarsely chopped
5   cups (1.25 liters) chicken stock

Serves: 4
Preparation: 15 minutes
Cooking: 25 minutes
Level: 1

WATERCRESS SOUP

Combine the watercress, onions, and stock in a large saucepan over medium heat. Bring to a boil. • Simmer gently for 10 minutes, or until the watercress is tender. • Purée with a hand-held blender or in a food processor. • Return to the heat and stir in the sour cream. • Season with cracked pepper to taste. Garnish with the extra sprigs of watercress and serve hot.

1 pound (500 g) watercress, + extra sprigs to garnish

2 onions, finely sliced

4 cups (1 liter) vegetable stock

3/4 cup (200 ml) sour cream

Cracked pepper

Serves: 4
Preparation: 10 minutes
Cooking: 15 minutes
Level: 1

TOMATO AND FENNEL SOUP

Trim the fennel, reserving a little of the leafy top leaves to garnish. • Finely slice one-third of the fennel bulbs and set aside. Coarsely chop the remainder. • Heat the butter in a large saucepan over low heat. • Add the coarsely chopped fennel and garlic and simmer for 10 minutes. • Increase the heat to medium-low and add the tomatoes. Simmer for 15 minutes, or until the tomatoes are soft and pulpy. • Purée with a hand-held blender or in a food processor. • Return to the heat and add the stock and finely sliced fennel. • Bring to a boil and simmer for 10 minutes, or until the fennel is tender. Garnish with the reserved fennel leaves and serve hot.

2 medium fennel bulbs, with leafy tops

3 tablespoons (45 g) butter

3 cloves garlic, finely chopped

3 pounds (1.5 kg) plum (roma) tomatoes, peeled and quartered

3 cups (750 ml) vegetable stock

Serves: 4
Preparation: 15 minutes
Cooking: 40 minutes
Level: 1

■ ■ ■ *Fresh tomatoes may be replaced with equal quantities of chopped canned tomatoes.*

LEEK AND POTATO SOUP

Melt the butter in a large saucepan over low heat. • Add the leeks and sauté for 5 minutes, or until softened. • Add the potatoes and sauté for 5 minutes. • Add the stock and bring to a boil. • Simmer for 15 minutes, or until the potatoes are tender. • Purée with a hand-held blender or in a food processor. • Reheat the soup for 2–3 minutes, garnish with the chives, and serve hot.

$1/3$ cup (90 g) butter

2 leeks, finely sliced

4 large potatoes, peeled and coarsely chopped

4 cups (1 liter) chicken stock

2 tablespoons chopped fresh chives or sprigs of fresh, flat-leaf parsley to garnish

Serves: 4
Preparation: 15 minutes
Cooking: 30 minutes
Level: 1

■ ■ ■ This is a variation on vichyssoise, the classic French soup.

SPLIT PEA SOUP

Combine all the ingredients in a large saucepan and bring to a boil. • Simmer gently for 1 hour. • Remove the hock, cut the meat from the bone, and cut into cubes. Set aside. • Purée the pea soup using a hand-held blender or in a food processor. • Return the meat to the soup and heat through. Serve hot.

2   cups (200 g) yellow split peas, rinsed

1   ham hock

1   large carrot, coarsely chopped

2   medium onions, coarsely chopped

4   cups (1 liter) chicken stock

Serves: 4
Preparation: 15 minutes
Cooking: 1 hour 10 minutes
Level: 1

CREAM OF MUSHROOM SOUP

Melt the butter in a large saucepan over low heat. • Simmer the mushrooms and thyme for 5 minutes. • Add the flour and stir for 2 minutes, or until smooth. • Gradually add the stock, stirring constantly to prevent lumps from forming. • Bring to a boil and simmer for 10 minutes. • Purée with a hand-held blender or in a food processor. • Reheat the soup for 2–3 minutes and serve hot.

1/4 cup (60 g) butter

14 ounces (400 g) mushrooms, sliced

1/3 cup (50 g) all-purpose (plain) flour

5 cups (1.25 liters) chicken stock

2 tablespoons finely chopped fresh thyme + extra sprigs to garnish

Serves: 4
Preparation: 10 minutes
Cooking: 20 minutes
Level: 1

COCONUT SHRIMP SOUP

Combine the curry paste and 1 cup (250 ml) of the fish stock in a large saucepan over medium heat. • Bring to a boil and simmer for 5 minutes. • Add the remaining 3 cups (750 ml) of stock, coconut milk, and lime juice. • Gently simmer for 5 minutes, but do not boil. • Add the shrimp and cook for 3–5 minutes, until shrimp are cooked and have changed color. • Serve hot.

1   teaspoon Thai green curry paste

4   cups (1 liter) fish stock

1   (14-ounce/400-ml) can coconut milk

1/4 cup (60 ml) freshly squeezed lime juice

16 large shrimp (green prawns), peeled and deveined

Serves: 4
Preparation: 10 minutes
Cooking: 15–20 minutes
Level: 1

■ ■ ■ *Thai green curry paste is available in Asian markets or the Asian foods section of your local supermarket.*

MISO SOUP
WITH SNOW PEAS

Combine the vegetable stock, miso paste, and carrot in a large saucepan over medium heat. • Bring to a boil and simmer very gently for 5 minutes. Do not boil again. • Add the snow peas and tofu and gently heat for 3 minutes. • Serve hot.

5 cups (1.25 liters) vegetable stock

5 tablespoons miso

1 carrot, julienned

16 snow peas (sugar peas/mangetout), trimmed and thinly sliced lengthwise

14 ounces (400 g) soft silken tofu, diced

Serves: 4
Preparation: 10 minutes
Cooking: 10 minutes
Level: 1

■ ■ ■ *Silken tofu has a soft, smooth texture and a high moisture content. Like all tofu (also known as bean curd and soybean curd), it is made from soy milk. Miso is a common ingredient in Japanese cooking, where it is used to thicken and flavor foods. Miso paste is available in several different varieties. They all work well in this recipe.*

SALADS

FRISÉE AND BACON SALAD

Slice the bacon into 1-inch (2.5-cm) strips. • Fry the bacon in a large frying pan over medium heat until crisp, then remove and set aside. • Fry the bread in the bacon fat until light golden brown and crisp. • Tear the frisée and transfer to a large bowl. • Peel and chop the eggs in half. • Add the eggs, bacon, bread, and vinegar to the lettuce. Toss gently and serve at once.

8 slices bacon
2 cups cubed bread
1 large head frisée lettuce or curly endive, leaves separated
4 eggs, soft boiled
¼ cup (60 ml) red wine or balsamic vinegar

Serves: 2–4
Preparation: 15 minutes
Cooking: 10 minutes
Level: 1

■■■ *This salad is best if served when the ingredients are still slightly warm. To obtain soft boiled eggs, with the whites firm enough to cut and the yolks still moist, lower the eggs into a pan of salted, boiling water and simmer uncovered for 10 minutes. Immediately plunge the eggs into cold water.*

PAPAYA AND WATERCRESS SALAD

Cut the papaya into quarters, remove the skin, and scoop out the seeds. • Slice into 3/4-inch (2-cm) thick pieces. • Combine the papaya and watercress in a large salad bowl. • Whisk the lime juice and sesame oil in a small bowl until well mixed. • Add the black sesame seeds and drizzle over the salad. • Toss well and serve at once.

1   large papaya

3   cups watercress

1/4   cup (60 ml) freshly squeezed lime juice

2   tablespoons (30 ml) Asian sesame oil

2   tablespoons black sesame seeds

Serves: 4
Preparation: 15 minutes
Level: 1

■ ■ ■ *Papaya is a pear-shaped tropical fruit native to the Americas but now cultivated in hot climates around the world.*

PROSCUITTO AND FIG SALAD

Whisk the balsamic vinegar and olive oil in a small bowl until well mixed. • Arrange the frisée, figs, and prosciutto on four serving plates. • Drizzle with the balsamic dressing. Serve at once.

5 tablespoons (75 ml) balsamic vinegar

1/4 cup (60 ml) extra-virgin olive oil

1 large head or 2 cups baby frisée or curly endive leaves

4 fresh figs, quartered

8 slices prosciutto

Serves: 4
Preparation: 10 minutes
Level: 1

■ ■ ■ *If preferred, replace the prosciutto in this salad with eight large slices of salami.*

WARM LENTIL SALAD

Preheat the oven to 350°F (180°C/gas 4). • Put the tomatoes on a baking sheet and drizzle with 1 tablespoon of the oil. Season with salt to taste. • Roast until softened, about 10 minutes. Remove and set aside. • Heat the remaining 3 tablespoons of oil in a medium saucepan over medium heat and add the lentils. • Cook until warmed through, about 5 minutes. • Combine the lentils and tomatoes, including any juices, in a large salad bowl. • Add the spinach leaves to the bowl and toss gently. The spinach should wilt a little. • Season with salt, if liked, and toss gently. • Serve at once.

8 ounces (250 g) cherry tomatoes

$1/4$ cup (60 ml) extra-virgin olive oil

Salt

$1^1/2$ cups (400 g) cooked or canned brown lentils, rinsed and drained

3 cups (150 g) baby spinach leaves

Serves: 4
Preparation: 10 minutes
Cooking: 15 minutes
Level: 1

SWEET ROASTED VEGETABLE SALAD

Preheat the oven to 400°F (220°C/gas 6). • Place the bell peppers on a baking sheet. • Roast until the skins begin to blister, about 30 minutes. • Remove the bell peppers from the oven and place in a small bowl. • Cover with plastic wrap (cling film) and allow to cool for 10 minutes. • Remove the seeds and skins from bell peppers under running cold water. • Slice into strips. • Slice the sweet potatoes into $3/4$-inch (2-cm) rounds. • Place on a baking sheet and drizzle with 1 tablespoon of the oil. • Roast until light brown and tender, about 15 minutes. • Combine the sweet potatoes, bell peppers, and arugula in a large salad bowl. • Add the remaining 3 tablespoons of oil and toss gently. • Divide the salad among four serving plates and top with the Parmesan. Serve at once.

3   red bell peppers (capsicums)
2   large sweet potatoes, peeled
1/4 cup (60 ml) extra-virgin olive oil
2   cups (100 g) arugula (rocket) leaves, washed
1/2 cup (60 g) Parmesan cheese, shaved

Serves: 4
Preparation: 25 minutes
Cooking: 45 minutes
Level: 1

SMOKED CHICKEN AND MANGO SALAD

Preheat the oven to 350°F (180°C/gas 4).
• Spread out the walnuts on a baking sheet and lightly roast for 5 minutes.
• Slice the smoked chicken and put into in a large bowl. • Cut the mangoes into 3/4-inch (2-cm) cubes and add to the chicken. • Add the frisée and walnuts to the chicken and toss well. • Add the vinegar and toss gently. Serve at once.

3/4 cup (90 g) walnuts

3 smoked chicken breasts

2 mangoes, peeled

3 cups (150 g) baby frisée or curly endive leaves

1/3 cup (90 ml) red wine vinegar

Serves: 4
Preparation: 15 minutes
Cooking: 5 minutes
Level: 1

EGGPLANT AND BELL PEPPER SALAD WITH PESTO DRESSING

Preheat the oven to 400°F (200°C/gas 6) • Place the bell peppers on a baking sheet. • Roast for 30 minutes or until the skin begins to blister all over. • Remove the bell peppers from the oven and place in a small bowl. • Cover with plastic wrap (cling film) and allow to cool for 10 minutes. • Remove the seeds and skins from the bell peppers under running cold water. • Slice into quarters lengthwise. • Place the eggplants on a baking sheet skin side down. Roast for 15 minutes, or until soft. • Combine the eggplants, bell peppers, and spinach in a large bowl. • Whisk the pesto and lemon juice in a small bowl until well mixed. • Drizzle over the salad and toss well. • Serve at once.

4 red bell peppers (capsicums)

8 baby eggplants (aubergine), halved lengthwise

3 cups (150 g) baby spinach

1/3 cup (90 g) pesto

1/3 cup (90 ml) freshly squeezed lemon juice

Serves: 4
Preparation: 20 minutes
Cooking: 45 minutes
Level: 2

WATERCRESS SALAD WITH FENNEL AND PANCETTA

Preheat the oven to 350°F (180°C/gas 4).
• Arrange the pancetta slices on a baking sheet in a single layer. Cook until crisp, about 8 minutes, then set aside. • Thinly slice the fennel lengthwise and put into in a large salad bowl. • Add the watercress and pancetta. • Peel and segment the oranges over a small bowl to collect the orange juice that drips as you work. Reserve for the dressing. Add the orange segments to the salad bowl.
• Whisk the orange juice and oil in a small bowl until well mixed. • Drizzle over the salad and toss gently.
• Serve at once.

20 slices pancetta

3 bulbs baby fennel, halved, cored

3 cups (150 g) watercress

2 oranges

1/3 cup (90 ml) extra-virgin olive oil

Serves: 4
Preparation: 20 minutes
Cooking: 8 minutes
Level: 1

BELGIAN ENDIVE AND BLUE CHEESE SALAD

Quarter the pears and remove the core. Slice each quarter into three and set aside. • Arrange the endives and pear slices on four serving plates. • Sprinkle with the cilantro and pieces of blue cheese. • Drizzle with the red wine vinegar. • Serve at once.

3   brown-skinned pears, such as Bosc

3   heads Belgian endive (wiltof), leaves separated

4   tablespoons fresh cilantro (coriander) leaves

8   ounces (250 g) soft blue cheese

1/3   cup (90 ml) red wine vinegar

Serves: 4
Preparation: 15 minutes
Level: 1

■ ■ ■ *If you are not serving this salad immediately, drizzle the slices of pear with a little freshly squeezed lemon juice to prevent them from turning brown.*

AVOCADO AND ORANGE SALAD

Using a large spoon, scoop out the avocado flesh. • Dice into $3/4$-inch (2-cm) pieces and put into a large bowl. • Add the watercress and pistachios. • Peel and segment the oranges over a bowl to collect the juice that drips as you work. Reserve for the dressing. Add the orange segments to the salad bowl. • Whisk the orange juice and olive oil in a small bowl until well mixed. • Drizzle over the salad and toss well. • Serve at once.

3   avocados, halved and pitted (stoned)

3   cups (150 g) watercress sprigs

$3/4$ cup (90 g) pistachios

3   oranges

$1/3$ cup (90 ml) extra-virgin olive oil

Serves: 4
Preparation: 20 minutes
Level: 1

TOASTED BREAD, PROSCUITTO, AND ASPARAGUS SALAD

Preheat the oven to 400°F (200°C/ gas 6). • Arrange the proscuitto on a baking sheet and bake until crisp, 10–15 minutes. • Set aside and reserve the fat. • Tear the bread into bite-sized pieces and put on a baking sheet. • Drizzle with the reserved fat and 1 tablespoon of oil, if necessary, to lightly coat each piece. • Bake for 15 minutes, or until crisp and golden brown. • Bring a large saucepan of salted water to a boil over high heat. • Blanch the asparagus for 3 minutes, or until tender. • Refresh in cold water to stop the cooking process. • Combine the asparagus, bread, and proscuitto in a large bowl. • Whisk the vinegar and remaining olive oil in a small bowl until well mixed. • Drizzle over the salad and toss well. • Serve at once.

12 slices proscuitto

1/2 loaf olive bread, crust removed

32 asparagus spears, woody ends removed and halved

1/3 cup (90 ml) extra-virgin olive oil

1/3 cup (90 ml) sherry vinegar

Serves: 4
Preparation: 15 minutes
Cooking: 28–33 minutes
Level: 1

SMOKED TROUT SALAD

Bring a medium saucepan of water to a boil over high heat. • Blanch the snowpeas for 2 minutes. • Refresh in cold water to stop the cooking process. • Combine the snow peas, bean sprouts, cherry tomatoes, and raspberry vinegar in a large bowl. • Flake the trout into bite-sized pieces and add to salad. Gently mix and serve at once.

2 cups (150 g) snow peas (sugar peas/ mangetout), trimmed and strings removed

1 cup (50 g) bean sprouts

1 pound (500 g) cherry tomatoes, halved

1/3 cup (90 ml) raspberry vinegar

1 smoked trout, halved and bones removed

Serves: 4
Preparation: 15 minutes
Cooking: 2 minutes
Level: 1

RADICCHIO AND APPLE SALAD

Cut the apples into quarters and remove the cores. • Slice each quarter into three pieces and put into a large salad bowl. • Drizzle with the sherry vinegar and toss gently. • Add the pistachios, radicchio, and feta. • Toss gently and serve at once.

2   crisp green apples (Granny Smiths are ideal)
$1/3$ cup (90 ml) sherry vinegar
$1/2$ cup (60 g) pistachios, roasted
2   small heads red radicchio, leaves separated
8   ounces (250 g) feta cheese, crumbled

Serves: 4
Preparation: 15 minutes
Level: 1

ORANGE, SNOW PEA, AND CASHEW SALAD

Bring a medium saucepan of water to a boil over high heat. • Blanch the snow peas for 2 minutes. • Refresh in cold water to stop the cooking process. • Combine the snow peas, spinach, and cashews in a large bowl. • Peel and segment the oranges over a bowl to collect the juice that drips as you work. Reserve for the dressing. Add the segments to the salad. • Whisk the orange juice and sesame oil in a small bowl until well mixed. • Drizzle over the salad and toss gently. • Serve at once.

$1^{1}/_{2}$ cups (100 g) snow peas (sugar peas/ mangetout), trimmed

3 cups (150 g) baby spinach leaves

$^{1}/_{2}$ cup (80 g) salted cashew nuts, toasted

2 oranges

3 tablespoons (45 ml) Asian sesame oil

Serves: 4
Preparation: 12 minutes
Cooking: 2 minutes
Level: 1

NEW POTATO SALAD

Bring a large pot of salted water to a boil over high heat. • Boil the potatoes until tender, 10–15 minutes (depending on the size of the potatoes). • Combine the yogurt, horseradish cream, and olive oil in a large bowl. • Drain the potatoes and add to the yogurt dressing, mixing well. • Cut the chives into 1-inch (2.5-cm) lengths. Add to the potatoes and toss gently. • Serve at once.

2   pounds (1 kg) small new potatoes

1/2   cup (125 g) plain yogurt

1/4   cup (60 ml) extra-virgin olive oil

1   tablespoon horseradish cream

1   bunch chives

Serves: 4–6
Preparation: 10 minutes
Cooking: 10–15 minutes
Level: 1

S A L A D S

MOZZARELLA, TOMATO, AND BASIL SALAD

Slice the mozzarella and tomatoes into ½-inch (1-cm) thick slices. • On four serving plates create layers of mozzarella and tomato. • Sprinkle the basil over the top. • Whisk the olive oil and balsamic vinegar together in a small bowl. • Drizzle over the salad. Serve at once.

8	ounces (250 g) fresh buffalo or cow's milk mozzarella
8	large ripe tomatoes
4	tablespoons finely chopped fresh basil
¼	cup (60 ml) extra-virgin olive oil
⅓	cup (90 ml) balsamic vinegar

Serves: 4
Preparation: 15 minutes
Level: 1

■ ■ ■ *This is a classic Italian salad. In its homeland it is known as a "caprese" after the beautiful island of Capri off the coast of Naples.*

LAMB SALAD WITH YOGURT

Heat the oil in a large frying pan over high heat. • Cook the lamb fillets for 4 minutes on each side for medium rare, or longer if desired. • Slice the tomatoes in half and combine with the arugula in a large bowl. • Slice the lamb and toss with the salad. • Divide the salad among four serving plates. Top each one with a dollop of yogurt. Serve warm.

3 tablespoons (45 ml) extra-virgin olive oil

1 pound (500 g) lamb tenderloin, sliced

8 ounces (250 g) cherry tomatoes

3 cups (150 g) arugula (rocket) leaves

3/4 cup (180 ml) plain Greek-style yogurt

Serves: 4
Preparation: 10 minutes
Cooking: 10 minutes
Level: 1

■ ■ ■ *This hearty salad can be thrown together in no time and and makes a delicious low-carb meal. If liked, add a peeled cubed cucumber and a teaspoon of finely chopped fresh mint leaves to the yogurt.*

CHICKEN WALDORF SALAD

Place a grill pan over medium-high heat. • Grill the chicken for 5 minutes on each side until cooked through. • Set aside and keep warm. • Slice the apple quarters into four and put in a large bowl. Add the watercress and walnuts and toss well. • Slice the chicken thinly and add to the salad. • Drizzle with the ranch dressing. • Serve at room temperature.

4   boneless, skinless chicken breasts

2   red apples, cored and cut into quarters

3   cups (150 g) watercress

1/2 cup (60 g) walnuts, toasted

1/2 cup (125 ml) ranch dressing

Serves: 4
Preparation: 10 minutes
Cooking: 10 minutes
Level: 1

EGG AND POTATO SALAD

Bring a large pot of water to a boil.
• Add the potatoes and boil for 7–10
minutes until tender. • Drain and let cool
completely. • Cook the eggs in a medium
saucepan of barely simmering water for
6 minutes. • Drain and let cool
completely. • Shell the eggs and cut
in half lengthwise. • Mix the potatoes,
eggs, walnuts, capers, and mayonnaise
in a large bowl. • Chill for 1 hour
and serve.

2   pounds (1 kg) new
    potatoes, cut in half

6   large eggs

1   cup (125 g) walnuts,
    toasted

2   tablespoons salt-
    cured capers, rinsed

3/4 cup (180 ml)
    mayonnaise

Serves: 4
Preparation: 15 minutes
    + 1 hour to chill
Cooking: 13–16 minutes
Level: 1

NIÇOISE SALAD

Cook the eggs in a medium saucepan of barely simmering water for 6 minutes. • Drain and let cool completely. • Shell the eggs and cut into quarters. • Blanch the green beans in a large saucepan of boiling water for 2 minutes. • Drain and rinse in ice-cold water to stop the cooking process. • Transfer to a large bowl. • Mix in the tuna, olives, and eggs. • Mix the lemon juice and oil reserved from the tuna in a small bowl. • Pour the dressing over the salad and toss well. • Serve at room temperature.

6 large eggs

8 ounces (250 g) green beans

2 cups (400 g) canned tuna in olive oil, with oil reserved

3/4 cup (80 g) black olives

1/3 cup (90 ml) freshly squeezed lemon juice

Serves: 4
Preparation: 10 minutes
Cooking: 8 minutes
Level: 1

■ ■ ■ *There are many variations on this classic salad. Feel free to experiment, but always keep the basic mix of tuna and eggs.*

GRAINS

TOMATO AND BASIL RISOTTO

Combine the tomatoes and stock in a medium saucepan. Bring to a boil and decrease the heat to keep it warm.
• Melt 2 tablespoons of the butter in a large, deep frying pan. • Add the rice and cook for 2 minutes, stirring constantly.
• Gradually add the tomato stock, $^1/_2$ cup (125 ml) at a time. Cook and stir until each addition has been absorbed and the rice is tender, 15–18 minutes. • Stir in the remaining 2 tablespoons of butter and chopped basil. Let stand for 5 minutes.
• Garnish with the basil leaves and serve hot.

2	(16-ounce/500-g) cans chopped tomatoes, with juice
3	cups (750 ml) vegetable stock
$^1/_4$	cup (60 g) butter, cut up
2	cups (400 g) risotto rice (Arborio, Carnaroli, Vialone nano)
5	tablespoons coarsely chopped fresh basil, plus whole leaves to garnish

Serves: 4
Preparation: 10 minutes
  + 5 minutes to stand
Cooking: 25 minutes
Level: 1

■ ■ ■ *Making risotto is easy, although it does require constant stirring during the cooking process so that the rice gradually releases its starches, and the risotto takes on its delicious, creamy consistency. The choice of rice is also important; if possible, always use an Italian superfino rice. We have suggested three of the best Italian risotto rices—Arborio, Carnaroli, and Vialone nano—which are all widely available in supermarkets and specialty food stores.*

SPINACH AND GORGONZOLA RISOTTO

Cook the spinach in a large pot of boiling water over medium heat for 7–10 minutes, until tender. • Drain, squeezing out the excess water, and transfer to a food processor or blender. Process until smooth, then set aside. • Melt 2 tablespoons of the butter in a large, deep frying pan. • Add the rice and cook for 2 minutes, stirring constantly. • Gradually add the stock, $1/2$ cup (125 ml) at a time. Cook and stir until each addition has been absorbed and the rice is tender, 15–18 minutes. • Mix in the puréed spinach and the remaining 2 tablespoons of butter. • Spoon the risotto into serving dishes and top with the Gorgonzola. Serve hot.

2 bunches spinach, tough stems removed

$1/4$ cup (60 g) butter, cut up

2 cups (400 g) risotto rice (Arborio, Carnaroli, Vialone nano)

4 cups (1 liter) chicken stock, heated

$1/2$ cup (125 g) Gorgonzola cheese or other soft blue cheese, cut into cubes

Serves: 4
Preparation: 5 minutes
Cooking: 25–30 minutes
Level: 1

SHRIMP AND SAFFRON RISOTTO

Combine the saffron and stock in a medium saucepan. Bring to a boil, then decrease the heat to keep it warm. • Melt 2 tablespoons of the butter in a large, deep frying pan. • Add the rice and cook for 2 minutes, stirring constantly. • Gradually add the saffron stock, $1/2$ cup (125 ml) at a time, stirring until each addition has been absorbed. • Add the shrimp with the last $1/2$ cup (125 ml) of stock. • Cook and stir until the rice is tender and the shrimp are pink and cooked. The whole process should take 15–18 minutes. • Stir in the remaining 2 tablespoons of butter and let stand for 5 minutes. Serve hot.

$1/4$ teaspoon crumbled saffron threads

4 cups (1 liter) fish stock

$1/4$ cup (60 g) butter, cut up

2 cups (400 g) risotto rice (Arborio, Carnaroli, Vialone Nano)

20 raw medium shrimp (prawns), shelled and deveined

Serves: 4
Preparation: 10 minutes
  + 5 minutes to stand
Cooking: 30 minutes
Level: 1

FRIED RICE WITH EGG

Bring a large saucepan of salted water to a boil. • Add the rice and cook over medium heat for 10–15 minutes, until tender. • Drain well and set aside. • Cook the mushrooms in a large nonstick frying pan over medium heat for 5 minutes, until lightly browned. • Add the rice, scallions, and soy sauce. Cook, stirring, for 4 minutes. • Set aside and keep warm. • Fry the eggs in a large nonstick frying pan over medium heat for 3 minutes. • Arrange the fried rice on individual serving plates and top with the fried eggs. • Serve hot.

2 cups (400 g) basmati rice
1 pound (500 g) button mushrooms, thinly sliced
4 scallions (spring onions), thinly sliced
1/3 cup (90 ml) soy sauce
4 large eggs

Serves: 4
Preparation: 10 minutes
Cooking: 22–27 minutes
Level: 1

SAVORY RICE

Bring a large saucepan of salted water to a boil. • Add the rice and cook over medium heat for 10–15 minutes, until tender. • Drain well and set aside.
• Cook the green beans in a small saucepan of boiling water for 4 minutes.
• Drain and set aside. • Dry-fry the pancetta in a large frying pan over medium heat for 5 minutes. • Add the garlic and cook for 1 minute. • Add the green beans and rice. • Cook, stirring often, for 5 minutes, until heated through. • Add the eggs and serve hot.

2   cups (400 g) basmati rice

12   ounces (350 g) green beans, trimmed

1¼ cups (150 g) diced pancetta

2   cloves garlic, finely chopped

6   hard-boiled eggs, shells removed and cut into quarters

Serves: 4
Preparation: 15 minutes
Cooking: 25–30 minutes
Level: 1

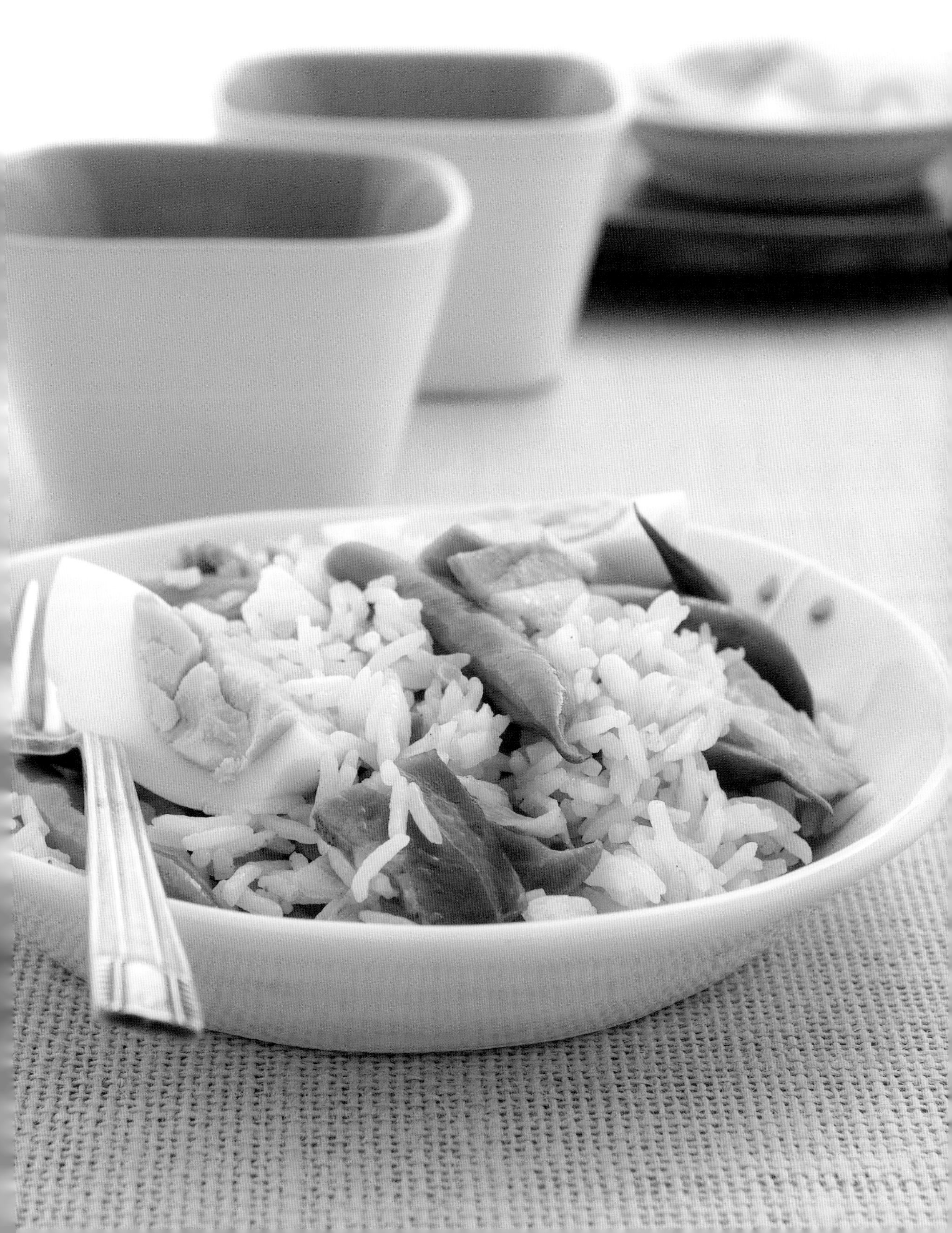

FRUITY WILD RICE

Bring a large saucepan of water to a boil.
• Add the rice and cook over medium
heat for about 40 minutes, or until
tender. • Drain well. • Grate the zest from
the oranges into a large bowl. • Peel and
segment the oranges, catching any drips.
Place the segments, and any juice, in the
bowl with the zest. • Mix in the cooked
rice, apricots, pistachios, and cilantro.
• Serve hot.

2 **cups (400 g) wild rice**

2 **oranges**

1/4 **cup (135 g) chopped dried apricots**

1/2 **cup (80 g) salted pistachio nuts, toasted**

3 **tablespoons finely chopped fresh cilantro (coriander)**

Serves: 4
Preparation: 15 minutes
Cooking: 40 minutes
Level: 1

COCONUT RICE

Mix the rice, coconut milk, and $2^2/3$ cups (400 ml) salted water in a medium saucepan. • Bring to a boil and simmer over low heat for 15–20 minutes, until the rice is cooked and all the liquid has been absorbed. • Remove from the heat and mix in the peanuts and cilantro. Season with cracked peper to taste. • Let rest for 5 minutes. • Fluff the rice with a fork and serve hot.

2	cups (400 g) basmati rice
$1^1/4$	cups (310 ml) coconut milk
$3/4$	cup (120 g) salted peanuts, toasted
4	tablespoons fresh cilantro (coriander) leaves
	Cracked pepper

Serves: 4
Preparation: 5 minutes
  + 5 minutes to rest
Cooking: 15–20 minutes
Level: 1

SPICY CHICKEN FRIED RICE

Bring a large saucepan of salted water to a boil. • Add the rice and cook over medium heat for 10–15 minutes, until tender. • Drain well and set aside.
• Heat 1½ teaspoons of chili paste in a nonstick frying pan. Pour in the beaten eggs. • When the bottom is just set, side a wooden spatula under the eggs to loosen them from the pan. Shake the pan with a rotating movement to spread.
• Cook until nicely browned on the underside and the top is set. • Remove from the heat and slice into strips.
• Fry the chicken with the remaining chili paste in the same frying pan for 5 minutes, until the chicken is cooked.
• Add the rice and cook for 4 minutes, until heated through. • Mix in the egg strips and scallions. • Serve hot.

2   cups (400 g) basmati rice
2   tablespoons mild or spicy Thai red chili paste
3   eggs, lightly beaten
8   ounces (250 g) boneless, skinless chicken breasts or thighs, cut into small pieces
4   scallions (spring onions), sliced on the diagonal

Serves: 4
Preparation: 10 minutes
Cooking: 25–30 minutes
Level: 2

POLISH-STYLE BUCKWHEAT

Sauté the onion in the oil in a large saucepan over medium heat for 2 minutes. • Add the buckwheat and toast for 2 minutes. • Pour in the egg and stir quickly until the egg is cooked and the grains are separate. • Meanwhile, heat the stock in a separate large pot. Bring to a boil and pour over the buckwheat. • Simmer, uncovered, over low heat for 10 minutes, or until tender. • Fluff the grains lightly with a fork and serve hot.

1	large onion, thinly sliced
3	tablespoons extra-virgin olive oil
2	cups (400 g) roasted buckwheat groats or kasha
2	eggs, lightly beaten
5	cups (1.25 liters) vegetable stock

Serves: 4
Preparation: 5 minutes
Cooking: 15 minutes
Level: 1

■ ■ ■ *Buckwheat groats, also known as kasha, are hulled buckwheat grains. They are sold both roasted and unroasted; unroasted kasha is pale and bland in flavor while the roasted grains are dark with a lovely earthy flavor.*

QUINOA WITH GRAPEFRUIT

Bring the stock to a boil in a medium saucepan. • Decrease the heat to low and stir in the quinoa. • Cover and simmer for 15–20 minutes, until all the liquid has been absorbed. • Remove from the heat and set aside, covered. • Peel the grapefruits and break into segments. • Fluff the quinoa with a fork. • Mix the quinoa, golden raisins, chives, and grapefruit segments in a large bowl. • Serve hot.

4   cups (1 liter) vegetable stock

2   cups (400 g) quinoa, rinsed

3   grapefruits

3/4 cup (135 g) golden raisins (sultanas)

2   tablespoons chives, cut into short lengths

Serves: 4
Preparation: 10 minutes
Cooking: 15–20 minutes
Level: 1

■ ■ ■ *This South American grain was the staple food of the Incas. Pronounced keen-wa, this light grain is an excellent source of plant protein, iron, potassium, magnesium, and lysine.*

PEARL BARLEY PILAF

Combine the barley, stock, and oil in a large saucepan. Bring to a boil.

• Cover and simmer over low heat for 30 minutes, until the barley is tender and all the liquid has been absorbed.

• Remove from the heat. • Strip the leaves from the cilantro and parsley stems. Discard the stems. Mix in the cilantro and parsley leaves. • Serve hot.

2 cups (400 g) pearl barley

6 cups (1.5 liters) chicken stock

$1/3$ cup (90 ml) extra-virgin olive oil

1 small bunch fresh cilantro (coriander)

1 small bunch fresh parsley

Serves: 4
Preparation: 10 minutes
Cooking: 30 minutes
Level: 1

■ ■ ■ *Deliciously chewy pearl barley makes a good base for a salad or it can be instead of rice.*

SPICED CURRANT COUSCOUS

Melt the butter in a medium saucepan.
• Add the currants and garam masala.
Cook over medium heat for 3 minutes.
• Pour in the stock and bring to a boil.
• Stir in the couscous. Cover and remove
from the heat. • Let stand for 10 minutes,
until the couscous has completely
absorbed the liquid. • Fluff the couscous
with a fork. Serve.

1	tablespoon butter
1/2	cup (90 g) currants
2	teaspoons garam masala
2	cups (500 ml) vegetable stock
2	cups (400 g) instant couscous

Serves: 4
Preparation: 5 minutes
    + 10 minutes to stand
Cooking: 5 minutes
Level: 1

■ ■ ■ *Although couscous is treated like a grain,*
it is actually a small granular pasta made of semolina.
Quick and easy to prepare, couscous has become
a staple on tables around the world.

STUFFED MINI PUMPKINS

Cut the top off each pumpkin and scoop out the seeds and fibers. Set the tops aside. • Dry-fry the bacon in a medium frying pan for 5 minutes, until crisp. • Set aside. • Bring the stock to a boil in a small saucepan. • Put the couscous in a medium bowl and pour in the hot stock. • Cover and let stand for 10 minutes, until the couscous has completely absorbed the liquid. • Mix in the bacon and pine nuts. • Fill the pumpkins with the couscous mixture and replace the pumpkin tops. • Line a large steamer with parchment paper, making holes in it so that the steam can come through. • Place the pumpkins on top of the paper and cover with a lid. • Place the steamer over a saucepan of boiling water. • Steam the pumpkins for 35–40 minutes, until they are tender. • Remove the lid and pumpkin tops. Fluff the couscous with a fork, replace the pumpkin tops, and serve hot.

4 Golden Nugget or other mini pumpkins, each weighing about $1^{1}/4$ pounds (600 g)

6 slices bacon, coarsely chopped

$1^{1}/2$ cups (375 ml) chicken stock

$1^{1}/2$ cups (300 g) instant couscous

$1/2$ cup (90 g) pine nuts, toasted

Serves: 4
Preparation: 20 minutes + 10 minutes to stand
Cooking: 40–45 minutes
Level: 2

SYRIAN-STYLE BULGUR

Put the bulgur in a large bowl and cover with the hot chicken stock. • Let stand for 30 minutes. • Drain well. • Mix in the red cabbage, mint, and pomegranate seeds. • Serve hot.

2   cups (400 g) bulgur wheat (cracked wheat)

4   cups (1 liter) chicken stock, hot

2   cups (150 g) shredded red cabbage

3   tablespoons coarsely chopped fresh mint

    Seeds from 1 pomegranate

Serves: 4
Preparation: 5 minutes
    + 30 minutes to stand
Level: 1

■ ■ ■ *Bulgur is wheat that has been steamed whole, then dried and cracked into grits. The steaming process involved in its preparation means that bulgur is precooked and easy to prepare.*

BAKED POLENTA

Bring the stock to a boil in a medium saucepan. • Gradually sprinkle in the polenta, stirring constantly with a wooden spoon to prevent lumps from forming. • Continue cooking over medium heat, stirring almost constantly, for about 15 minutes, or until the polenta is thick and starts to pull away from the sides of the pan. • Remove from the heat. • Stir in the sun-dried tomatoes, 3/4 cup (90 g) of the Parmesan, and basil. • Pour the mixture into a 12-inch (30-cm) nonstick springform pan. • Spread the mixture evenly, pressing it down with the back of a spoon. • Let cool for 10 minutes. • Loosen and remove the pan sides and sprinkle with the remaining 3 tablespoons of Parmesan. • Broil (grill) for 5 minutes, until warmed through. • Slice into wedges and serve.

4 cups (1 liter) chicken stock

1 cup (150 g) instant polenta

1 cup (150 g) sun-dried tomatoes, finely chopped

3/4 cup (90 g) + 3 tablespoons freshly grated Parmesan cheese

3 tablespoons finely chopped fresh basil

Serves: 4–6
Preparation: 10 minutes
   + 10 minutes to cool
Cooking: 20 minutes
Level: 2

PASTA

SPAGHETTI WITH ANCHOVIES AND BLACK OLIVES

Cook the spaghetti in a large pot of salted boiling water until al dente.
• Sauté the anchovies and olives in the oil in a large frying pan over medium heat for 3 minutes. • Add the parsley and cook for 2 minutes. • Remove from the heat. • Drain the spaghetti and add to the pan with the anchovies. • Toss well and serve hot.

1   pound (500 g) dried spaghetti

16   anchovies, cleaned and cut in half lengthwise

1   cup (100 g) pitted (stoned) black olives

1/4   cup (60 ml) extra-virgin olive oil

1   cup (50 g) coarsely chopped fresh parsley

Serves: 4
Preparation: 5 minutes
Cooking: 15 minutes
Level: 1

SPINACH AND RICOTTA CANNELLONI WITH TOMATO SAUCE

Preheat the oven to 350°F (180°C/gas 4).
• Cook the spinach in a large pot of
boiling water for 1 minute. • Drain well.
• Coarsely chop the spinach and place in
a large bowl. • Mix in the ricotta and
nutmeg until well combined. • Use a
pastry bag fitted with a $^{1}/_{2}$-inch (1-cm)
tip to fill the cannelloni tubes with the
spinach and ricotta mixture. • Arrange
the filled cannelloni in a shallow baking
dish and pour the tomatoes over the top.
• Bake, uncovered, for about 40 minutes,
or until the pasta is al dente. • Serve hot.

2 pounds (1 kg)
   spinach leaves,
   tough stems
   removed

$1^{1}/_{2}$ cups (375 g) fresh
   ricotta cheese

2 teaspoons freshly
   grated nutmeg

12 dried cannelloni
   tubes

3 cups (750 g) peeled
   plum tomatoes,
   pressed through a
   fine-mesh strainer
   (passata)

Serves: 4
Preparation: 20 minutes
Cooking: 40 minutes
Level: 1

LINGUINE WITH BLUE CHEESE AND WALNUTS

Cook the linguine in a large pot of salted boiling water until al dente. • Drain well and return to the pan. • Heat the apple cider vinegar and walnuts in a medium saucepan. • Pour the mixture over the linguine and add the spinach and blue cheese. • Toss well and serve hot.

1   pound (500 g) dried linguine

$1/3$ cup (80 ml) apple cider vinegar

1   cup (125 g) walnuts, toasted

10   ounces (300 g) baby spinach leaves, tough stems removed

$1^1/4$ cups (210 g) soft blue cheese (such as Roquefort or Gorgonzola), crumbled

Serves: 4
Preparation: 5 minutes
Cooking: 15 minutes
Level: 1

BUCATINI WITH SMOKED SALMON

Cook the bucatini in a large pot of salted boiling water until al dente. • Cook the cream with the capers in a large frying pan over low heat for 4 minutes. • Stir in the smoked salmon and dill and simmer for 2 minutes. • Remove from the heat. • Drain the bucatini and add to the pan with the sauce. • Toss well. Garnish with the dill leaves and serve hot.

1 pound (500 g) dried bucatini or spaghetti

1¼ cups (310 ml) light (single) cream

3 tablespoons salt-cured capers, rinsed

8 ounces (250 g) smoked salmon, coarsely chopped

1 tablespoon finely chopped fresh dill leaves, plus dill leaves to garnish

Serves: 4
Preparation: 8 minutes
Cooking: 20 minutes
Level: 1

ORECCHIETTE WITH BROCCOLI AND PINE NUTS

Cook the orecchiette in a large pot of salted boiling water until al dente. • Cook the broccoli in a medium saucepan of boiling water for 5 minutes. • Drain and rinse in ice-cold water to stop the cooking process. • Mix the crème fraîche and pesto in a large frying pan and warm over low heat for 2 minutes. • Add the broccoli and pine nuts and cook for 1 minute. • Remove from the heat. • Drain the orecchiette and add to the pan with the sauce. • Toss well and serve hot.

1 pound (500 g) dried orecchiette

10 ounces (300 g) broccoli florets

1 cup (250 ml) crème fraîche or sour cream

3 tablespoons store-bought basil pesto

3/4 cup (135 g) pine nuts, toasted

Serves: 4
Preparation: 10 minutes
Cooking: 20 minutes
Level: 1

PAPPARDELLE WITH CHORIZO SAUSAGE

Cook the pappardelle in a large pot of salted boiling water until al dente.
• Dry-fry the chorizo in a large frying pan over medium heat for 5 minutes until crispy. • Stir in the tomatoes and cook for 4 minutes until softened. • Remove from the heat. • Drain the pappardelle and add to the pan with the chorizo.
• Add the parsley and toss well. • Sprinkle with the Parmesan and serve hot.

1 pound (500 g) dried pappardelle

8 ounces (250 g) Spanish chorizo sausage, thickly sliced

12 plum tomatoes, coarsely chopped

2 tablespoons coarsely chopped fresh parsley

1/2 cup (60 g) freshly grated Parmesan cheese

Serves: 4
Preparation: 10 minutes
Cooking: 20 minutes
Level: 1

PENNE WITH SMOKED CHICKEN AND PEAS

Cook the penne in a large pot of salted boiling water until al dente. • Warm the crème fraîche and chicken in a large frying pan over low heat for 4 minutes. • Add the peas and cook for 2 minutes. • Remove from the heat. • Drain the penne and add to the pan with the sauce. Season with black pepper. • Toss well and serve hot.

1   pound (500 g) penne

1   cup (250 ml) crème fraîche or sour cream

10 ounces (300 g) cooked smoked chicken breast, coarsely shredded

1   cup (125 g) fresh or frozen and thawed peas

Freshly ground black pepper

Serves: 4
Preparation: 10 minutes
Cooking: 20 minutes
Level: 1

ANGEL HAIR PASTA WITH PESTO AND TOMATOES

178

Cook the pasta in a large pot of salted boiling water until al dente. • Cook the cherry tomatoes with the pesto in a large frying pan over medium heat for 4 minutes, until the tomatoes begin to soften. • Remove from the heat. • Drain the pasta and add to the pan with the tomatoes. • Add the goat cheese and season with black pepper. • Toss well and serve hot.

1 pound (500 g) dried angel hair pasta or cappellini

10 ounces (300 g) cherry tomatoes

1/2 cup (125 ml) store-bought basil pesto

3/4 cup (180 g) crumbled soft goat cheese

Freshly ground black pepper

Serves: 4
Preparation: 5 minutes
Cooking: 10 minutes
Level: 1

LINGUINE WITH SCALLOPS AND LEMON

Cook the linguine in a large pot of salted boiling water until al dente. • Heat the basil and lemon zest in the oil in a large frying pan over low heat for 2 minutes. • Increase the heat to medium high, add the scallops, and sear them for 2 minutes on each side. • Add the lemon juice and warm through. • Remove from the heat. • Drain the linguine and add to the pan with the scallops. • Toss well and serve hot.

1	**pound (500 g) dried linguine**
1	**small bunch fresh basil, stems removed**
	Finely shredded zest and juice of 2 lemons
$1/3$	**cup (90 ml) extra-virgin olive oil**
1	**pound (500 g) scallops, cleaned and patted dry**

Serves: 4
Preparation: 15 minutes
Cooking: 15 minutes
Level: 1

FETTUCCINE WITH SHRIMP AND OREGANO

Cook the pasta in a large pot of salted boiling water until al dente. • Cook the capers and oregano in the oil in a large frying pan over low heat for 3 minutes. • Add the shrimp and cook for 4 minutes, turning them over, until they are pink and cooked through. • Remove from the heat. • Drain the pasta and add to the pan with the shrimp. • Toss well and serve hot.

1 pound (500 g) dried fettuccine or other long ribbon pasta

2 tablespoons salt-cured capers, rinsed

5 tablespoons fresh oregano sprigs

1/3 cup (90 ml) extra-virgin olive oil

20 raw shrimps (prawns), shelled, heads removed, and deveined

Serves: 4
Preparation: 20 minutes
Cooking: 10 minutes
Level: 1

FARFALLE WITH ARTICHOKES AND ROASTED PEPPERS

Broil (grill) the bell peppers until the skins are blackened all over. • Wrap them in a paper bag for 5 minutes, then remove the skins and seeds. Slice into strips. • Cook the farfalle in a large pot of salted boiling water until al dente.
• Combine the bell peppers, artichokes, and olives in a large frying pan and heat until warmed through. • Drain the farfalle and add to the pan with the sauce. Add the spinach. • Toss well and serve hot.

2   red bell peppers (capsicums)

1   pound (500 g) dried farfalle

5   ounces (150 g) marinated artichoke hearts, cut into quarters

$1/2$ cup (50 g) pitted (stoned) black olives

8   ounces (250 g) baby spinach leaves, tough stems removed

Serves: 4
Preparation: 20 minutes
   + 5 minutes to rest
Cooking: 20 minutes
Level: 1

PAPPARDELLE WITH PANCETTA AND ARUGULA

Cook the pappardelle in a large pot of salted boiling water until al dente. • Dry-fry the pancetta in a large frying pan over medium heat for 3 minutes, until crispy. • Add the tomatoes and cook for 3 minutes. • Drain the pappardelle and add to the pan with the pancetta and tomatoes. • Add the arugula and Parmesan. • Toss well and serve hot.

1	pound (500 g) dried pappardelle
20	slices pancetta or bacon
1	pound (500 g) cherry tomatoes, cut in half
2	cups (100 g) arugula (rocket) leaves
1/2	cup (60 g) shaved Parmesan cheese

Serves: 4
Preparation: 5 minutes
Cooking: 20 minutes
Level: 1

PENNE WITH SWEET POTATOES AND FETA

Preheat the oven to 400°F (200°C/ gas 6). • Place the sweet potatoes on a baking sheet and drizzle with 2 tablespoons of the oil. • Bake for about 15 minutes, or until softened. • Cook the penne in a large pot of salted boiling water until al dente. • Drain well and return to the pan. • Sauté the leeks in the remaining 2 tablespoons of oil in a large frying pan over medium heat for 3 minutes. • Stir in the penne, sweet potatoes, and feta. • Toss well and serve hot.

2   sweet potatoes, peeled and diced

1/4   cup (60 ml) rosemary-infused olive oil

1   pound (500 g) dried penne

2   leeks, thinly shredded

6   ounces (180 g) marinated feta cheese

Serves: 4
Preparation: 10 minutes
Cooking: 25 minutes
Level: 1

SPAGHETTI MARINARA

Cook the spaghetti in a large pot of salted boiling water until al dente.
• Combine the tomatoes, olives, and garlic in a medium saucepan over low heat and cook for 5 minutes. • Add the seafood and cook over low heat for about 5 minutes, or until the seafood is cooked.
• Drain the spaghetti and add to the pan with the seafood sauce. • Toss well and serve hot.

1   **pound (500 g) dried spaghetti**

3   **cups (750 g) peeled and chopped tomatoes, with juice**

1/2 **cup (50 g) pitted (stoned) black olives, coarsely chopped**

3   **cloves garlic, finely chopped**

12 **ounces (350 g) mixed seafood (mussels, clams etc.)**

Serves: 4
Preparation: 5 minutes
Cooking: 20 minutes
Level: 1

■ ■ ■ *You can use fresh or frozen mixed seafood for this recipe. If using frozen seafood, make sure that you thaw the mixture before cooking.*

PASTA WITH CREAMY SUN-DRIED TOMATO SAUCE

Cook the pasta in a large pot of salted boiling water until al dente. • Combine the sun-dried tomatoes, onion, and cream in a large frying pan and cook over low heat for 5 minutes. • Add the Parmesan and cook for 2 minutes.
• Drain the pasta and add to the pan with the sauce. • Toss well and serve hot.

1   pound (500 g) large elbow macaroni (pipe rigate)

12 sun-dried tomatoes, finely chopped

1   large onion, finely chopped

1¼ cups (310 ml) light (single) cream

½   cup (60 g) freshly grated Parmesan cheese

Serves: 4
Preparation: 8 minutes
Cooking: 20 minutes
Level: 1

FETTUCCINE ALFREDO

Cook the fettuccine in a large pot of salted boiling water until al dente. • Melt the butter in a large frying pan. • Add the cream and Parmesan and cook over low heat for 4 minutes. • Stir in the parsley. • Drain the fettuccine and add to the pan with the sauce. • Toss well and serve hot.

1 pound (500 g) dried fettuccine

$1/3$ cup (90 g) butter, cut up

$1^1/4$ cups (310 ml) light (single) cream

$1/2$ cup (60 g) freshly grated Parmesan cheese

3 tablespoons finely chopped fresh parsley

Serves: 4
Preparation: 5 minutes
Cooking: 15 minutes
Level: 1

LINGUINE CARBONARA

Cook the linguine in a large pot of salted boiling water until al dente. • Fry the bacon in a large frying pan over medium heat for 3 minutes, until crispy. Set aside. • Beat the eggs with the cream and Parmesan in a medium bowl. • Add the bacon. • Drain the linguine and return to the pan. Pour in the egg mixture and cook over very low heat for 2 minutes, until the sauce begins to thicken and the eggs are cooked through. • Toss well and serve hot.

1 pound (500 g) dried linguine

8 slices bacon, thinly sliced

4 large eggs

$1^{1}/_{4}$ cups (310 ml) light (single) cream

$^{1}/_{2}$ cup (60 g) freshly grated Parmesan cheese

Serves: 4
Preparation: 10 minutes
Cooking: 15 minutes
Level: 1

■ ■ ■ *Carbonara is a classic pasta sauce in modern Roman cuisine. It first appeared at the end of World War II, and many believe that it was invented in the Eternal City when Allied troops arrived and began dispensing their military rations—of which bacon and eggs were key elements.*

SEAFOOD

STUFFED MUSSELS

Preheat the oven to 400°F (200°C/gas 6). • Combine the bread crumbs, cheese, parsley, anchovies, and reserved oil in a medium bowl. • Open the mussels by inserting a short strong knife or oyster shucker near the hinge and twist to open the shell. Discard the top shells. • Place the mussels on a baking sheet and cover each one with about 1 tablespoon of the bread crumb mixture. • Bake for 10–12 minutes. • Serve hot.

$1^1/2$ cups (100 g) fresh bread crumbs

$1/4$ cup (50 g) freshly grated Parmesan cheese

1 cup (50 g) finely chopped fresh parsley

4 anchovy fillets, preserved in oil, $1/4$ cup (60 ml) of the oil reserved

24 mussels, in shells, cleaned and beards removed

Serves: 2
Preparation: 20 minutes + time to clean mussels
Cooking: 10–12 minutes
Level: 1

SCALLOP CEVICHE

Take the scallops off the shells. Reserve the shells. • Remove the white membrane from scallops using a small knife. • Place the scallops in a medium nonreactive bowl. • Add the lime juice, zest, chile, and cilantro. • Stir to combine well. • Cover and refrigerate for 1 hour, or until the scallops begin to turn from opaque to white. • Place the scallops back on the shells and drizzle the dressing in the bowl over the top. • Season with cracked pepper and serve.

16 **scallops, in half shells**
8 **limes, juiced + 1 tablespoon finely chopped lime zest**
1 **large green chile, seeded and finely diced**
3 **tablespoons finely chopped fresh cilantro (coriander)**
Cracked pepper

Serves: 2
Preparation: 15 minutes + 1 hr to chill
Level: 1

SHRIMP AND MANGO SALAD

Combine the mayonnaise and lime juice in a large bowl. • Add the shrimp and mangoes and stir well to combine. • Coarsely shred the lettuce and divide among four serving bowls. If preferred, use whole leaves. • Divide the shrimp mixture among the bowls on top of the lettuce and serve.

$3/4$ cup (180 ml) mayonnaise

$1/4$ cup (60 ml) freshly squeezed lime juice

$1^1/2$ pounds (750 g) cooked shrimp (prawn), peeled and deveined

2 mangoes, peeled and diced

1 small head romaine (cos) lettuce

Serves: 4
Preparation: 15 minutes
Level: 1

PAN-FRIED SALMON WITH GRAPEFRUIT SALAD

Combine the dill and 3 tablespoons (45 ml) of the oil in a small bowl. • Place a large frying pan on high heat. • Coat the salmon in the dill oil and place in the hot pan, skin side down. Cook two fillets at a time so that pan retains its heat. • Cook for 2–3 minutes on each side; the salmon should still be a little translucent inside. • Combine the watercress, grapefruit, reserved juice, and the remaining 1 tablespoon of oil in a medium bowl. • Divide the fish and salad evenly among four serving plates. • Serve hot.

4   tablespoons finely chopped fresh dill

1/4 cup (60 ml) extra-virgin olive oil

4   (8-ounce/250 g) salmon fillets

3   cups (150 g) watercress sprigs

2   pink grapefruit, peeled and segmented, juice reserved

Serves: 4
Preparation: 10 minutes
Cooking: 8–12 minutes
Level: 1

■ ■ ■ *If you live in Australia, substitute ocean trout for the salmon, if preferred.*

BAKED SALMON WITH THYME POTATOES

Preheat the oven to 400°F (200°C/gas 6). • Put the potatoes in a large saucepan of salted boiling water. Cook for 3–4 minutes, or until just tender. Drain well. • Combine the potatoes, half the oil and half the thyme in a large ovenproof dish. • Mix gently to coat the potatoes with oil and bake for 25–30 minutes. • Pour the remaining oil into a large frying pan over high heat. • Cook the salmon fillets for 1 minute on each side. • Place the salmon on top of the potatoes, sprinkle with the capers, and bake for 8–10 minutes, or until the salmon is just cooked. • Divide the potatoes evenly among four serving plate and top with the salmon. • Serve hot.

2 pounds (1 kg) potatoes, peeled and thickly sliced

1/3 cup (90 ml) extra-virgin olive oil

12 fresh thyme sprigs

4 (6-ounce/180-g) salmon fillets, skin removed

1/4 cup (50 g) salt-cured capers, rinsed

Serves: 4
Preparation: 5 minutes
Cooking: 40–45 minutes
Level: 1

BAKED SEA BASS WITH CAPERS AND LEMON

Preheat the oven 350°F (180°C/gas 4). • Line a large baking sheet with aluminum foil. • Place the sea bass on the foil, sprinkle with the capers, and cover with the slices of lemon. • Cover with foil, so that fish is entirely encased and the juices will not spill out during cooking. • Bake for 12–15 minutes. • Combine the arugula and tomato in a medium bowl and toss to combine. • Divide the fish and salad evenly among four serving plates. • Serve hot.

4   (8-ounce/250-g) sea bass (barramundi) fillets or steaks

2   lemons, thinly sliced, with peel

2   tablespoons salt-cured capers, rinsed

3   cups (150 g) arugula (rocket) leaves

4   large tomatoes, diced

Serves: 4
Preparation: 5 minutes
Cooking: 12–15 minutes
Level: 1

■ ■ ■ *You will need a large, firm-fleshed fish to make this recipe. Some good alternatives (depending on where you live) are red snapper, croaker, halibut, grouper, monkfish, trevally, hapuku, mako shark, or rockfish.*

CRUMBED FISH WITH TARTAR SAUCE

Put the bread crumbs on a large plate or tray. • Press the fish fillets into the bread crumbs so that they are thoroughly coated; set aside. • Heat the oil in a large frying pan over medium heat. • Cook the fish for 3 minutes on each side, or until the flesh flakes easily and the crumbs are golden. • Place the fish and salad greens on four serving plates. Spoon the tartar sauce into four small bowls, one for each plate. • Serve hot.

1½ cups (90 g) fresh bread crumbs

4 (8-ounce/250 g) fillets firm white fish, such as snapper, John Dory, whiting, blue-eye, cod, flounder, grouper, halibut

½ cup (125 ml) canola oil

3 cups (150 g) mixed salad greens

¾ cup (180 ml) tartar sauce

Serves: 4
Preparation: 5 minutes
Cooking: 6 minutes
Level: 1

GRILLED TUNA WITH WATERMELON SALAD

Combine the watercress, watermelon, and 1 tablespoon (15 ml) of the oil in a medium bowl. • Toss to combine well and divide among four serving plates. • Heat a barbecue grill to medium-high heat. • Coat the tuna with the remaining 2 tablespoons of oil and cook for 2 minutes on each side; the tuna should still be pink inside. • Place the tuna on the salad and top with cracked pepper to taste. • Serve hot.

1 cup (50 g) watercress sprigs

2 cups (400 g) cubed watermelon

3 tablespoons (45 ml) lemon-infused olive oil

4 (8-ounce/250-g) tuna steaks, cut about 1 inch (2.5 cm) thick

Cracked pepper

Serves: 4
Preparation: 10 minutes
Cooking: 4 minutes
Level: 1

CEVICHE WITH MANGO

Cut the fish into $^3/_4$-inch (2-cm) pieces and put into a medium bowl. • Add the mango, chiles, lime juice, and zest and stir well to combine. • Cover the bowl and refrigerate for 1 hour, or until fish turns from opaque to white. • Season to taste with salt and serve.

2 pounds (1 kg) skinless firm white fish fillets, such as flounder, snapper, grouper, cod, or trevalla

1 large mango, peeled and diced

3 small red chiles, seeded and finely chopped

8 limes, juiced + 1 tablespoon finely chopped lime zest

Sea salt

Serves: 4
Preparation: 15 minutes
  + 1 hour to chill
Level: 1

S E A F O O D

218

GRILLED SNAPPER WITH FRESH TOMATO SALSA

Preheat a barbecue grill or grill pan over medium-high heat. • Score the snapper with a sharp knife, making three cuts on each side. • Rub the fish with the olive oil. • Grill for 10 minutes on each side, or until the skin becomes crisp and the flesh flakes easily. (Cooking time will vary depending on the size of the fish.) • Mix the tomatoes, onion, and vinegar in a medium bowl. Spoon over the cooked fish. • Serve hot.

1 whole snapper, 4–6 pounds (2–3 kg), scaled, cleaned, and fins trimmed

1/4 cup (60 ml) infused olive oil (chile or herb)

1 1/4 pounds (600 g) cherry tomatoes, halved

1 large red onion, diced

1/4 cup (60 ml) balsamic vinegar

Serves: 4
Preparation: 10 minutes
Cooking: 20 minutes
Level: 1

BAKED FISH STEAKS WITH ROASTED TOMATOES

Preheat the oven to 400°F (200°C/gas 6). • Combine the tomatoes and olives in a medium baking dish and drizzle with half the oil. Bake for 5 minutes. • Add the fish and bake for 10–15 minutes, or until the flesh flakes easily. • Remove the fish and keep warm. • Stir the arugula through the roasted tomatoes and olives. Divide evenly among four serving dishes and place the fish on top. • Serve hot.

6   plum (roma) tomatoes, halved
1/2 cup (50 g) black olives
1/3 cup (90 ml) extra-virgin olive oil
4   (8-ounce/250 g) firm white fish steaks, such as cod, snapper, ling, or warehou, cut about 3/4 inch (2 cm) thick
2   cups (100 g) arugula (rocket) leaves

Serves: 4
Preparation: 5 minutes
Cooking: 15–20 minutes
Level: 1

JAPANESE-STYLE FISH

Mix the miso and mirin in a small bowl.
• Rub the miso marinade over the fish
and refrigerate for 2 hours. • Bring a
large saucepan of water to a boil. • Add
the rice and cook until tender, about
10–15 minutes. • Drain and set aside.
• Preheat a grill pan over medium-high
heat. • Cook the fish for 3 minutes on
each side, or until the flesh flakes easily.
• Divide the fish and rice evenly among
four serving bowls or plates. Top with the
pickled ginger. • Serve hot.

$1/4$ cup (60 ml) miso

$1/4$ cup (60 ml) mirin
(Japanese cooking
wine)

8 (3-ounce/90 g)
pieces firm white
fish, such as
snapper, John Dory,
whiting, cod

$1^1/2$ cups (300 g)
basmati rice

$1/2$ cup (100 g) pickled
ginger

Serves: 4
Preparation: 10 minutes
+ 2 hours to marinate
Cooking: 20–25 minutes
Level: 1

■ ■ ■ *Pickled ginger, also known as gari or sushoga*
(from the Japanese), is ginger preserved in rice
vinegar, brine, or red wine. It is sweet and
slightly spicy.
Mirin is a low-alcohol Japanese rice wine. It is not
always easy to find, but you can make a reasonable
substitute by bringing $1/4$ cup (50 g) sugar to a boil
with 2–3 tablespoons water. Let cool, then stir in about
$2/3$ cup (150 ml) good-quality sake.

CAJUN FISH WITH GRILLED LEMON

Brush the fish with $1/4$ cup (60 g) of butter and coat in the Cajun spices.
• Place a large frying pan over medium-high heat. • Drizzle with a little butter.
• Cook the fish for 2 minutes on each side, or until flesh flakes easily. Add the remaining butter as you turn the fish.
• Place a small frying pan over high heat.
• Grill the lemons flesh side down for 1 minute, or until colored. • Serve the fish hot with the spinach and grilled lemon.

4 (8-ounce/250-g) white fish fillets, such as cod, snapper, ling, or warehou

$1/2$ cup (125 g) butter, melted

2 tablespoons Cajun spice mix

3 cups (150 g) baby spinach leaves

2 lemons, halved

Serves: 4
Preparation: 5–10 minutes
Cooking: 5 minutes
Level: 1

PESTO FISH WITH ORANGE AND OLIVE SALAD

Heat a large nonstick frying pan over medium-high heat. • Coat the fish in the pesto and cook for 3 minutes on each side, or until the flesh flakes easily.
• Combine the arugula, orange segments, and olives in a medium bowl. • Divide the salad and fish evenly among four serving plates. • Serve hot.

4   (8-ounce/250-g) firm white fish fillets, such as red mullet, John Dory, sea bass, hapuku, cod, ling, halibut, flounder, pollock, monkfish, grouper, rockfish, or tilapia

1/2 cup (125 g) basil pesto

3   cups (150 g) arugula (rocket) leaves

4   oranges, peeled and segmented

3/4 cup (75 g) black olives

Serves: 4
Preparation: 5 minutes
Cooking: 6 minutes
Level: 1

CHICKEN

GLAZED APRICOT CHICKEN

Preheat the oven to 350°F (180°C/gas 4).
• Combine the apricots and juice, chicken stock, and apple cider vinegar in a medium saucepan and bring to a boil.
• Arrange the chicken breasts in a baking dish in a single layer and pour in the apricot mixture. • Bake for 10 minutes.
• Remove from the oven and baste with the juices. Bake for 15 minutes, basting the chicken every 5 minutes. • Remove the chicken from the oven and set aside.
• Bring a large saucepan of salted water to a boil. • Add the rice and cook over medium heat for 10–15 minutes until tender. • Drain well. • Arrange the rice on serving plates, topped with the chicken and sauce. • Serve hot.

1   (14-ounce/400-g) can apricot halves, with half the juice reserved
1   cup (250 ml) chicken stock
1   tablespoon apple cider vinegar
4   boneless, skinless chicken breasts
1¹/2 cups (300 g) basmati rice

Serves: 4
Preparation: 10 minutes
Cooking: 35–40 minutes
Level: 1

TERIYAKI CHICKEN WINGS

Put the chicken wings in a large bowl and cover with the teriyaki sauce. Cover with plastic wrap (cling film) and refrigerate for 1 hour. • Combine the tomatoes and cilantro in a medium bowl and mix well. • Bring a large saucepan of salted water to a boil. • Add the rice and cook over medium heat for 10–15 minutes until tender. • Drain well and keep warm. • Place a grill pan over medium-high heat. • Grill the chicken for 5 minutes on each side until cooked through. • Serve the chicken hot with the tomatoes and rice.

20 chicken wings

$^3/_4$ cup (180 ml) teriyaki sauce

6 tomatoes, coarsely chopped

3 tablespoons fresh cilantro (coriander) leaves

$1^1/_2$ cups (300 g) basmati rice

Serves: 4
Preparation: 10 minutes
  + 1 hour to marinate
Cooking: 20–25 minutes
Level: 1

SPICY SWEET CHICKEN

Coat the chicken with the honey and sambal oelek in a large bowl. • Cover with plastic wrap (cling film) and refrigerate for 1 hour. • Mix the spinach and tomatoes in a medium bowl. • Place a grill pan over medium-high heat. • Grill the chicken for 5 minutes on each side, until cooked through. • Serve the chicken hot with the salad.

4 boneless, skinless chicken breasts

1/2 cup (125 ml) honey

1/4 cup (60 ml) sambal oelek

3 cups (150 g) baby spinach leaves

8 ounces (250 g) cherry tomatoes, halved

Serves: 4
Preparation: 10 minutes
+ 1 hour to marinate
Cooking: 10 minutes
Level: 1

■ ■ ■ *Sambal oelek is a very spicy sauce made from chile peppers. Used in Indonesia and Malaysia as a condiment and available online, it can be replaced with minced fresh peppers.*

TANDOORI DRUMSTICKS

Use a sharp knife to make deep cuts all over the drumsticks. • Mix the yogurt, tandoori paste, and lemon juice in a large bowl. • Coat the drumsticks with the mixture. Cover with plastic wrap (cling film) and refrigerate for 1 hour. • Place a grill pan over medium-high heat. • Grill the drumsticks for 15 minutes, turning them often, until cooked through. • Serve the drumsticks hot with the arugula.

8   chicken drumsticks

$2/3$ cup (150 ml) plain yogurt

3   tablespoons tandoori paste

Freshly squeezed juice of 1 lemon

3   cups (150 g) arugula (rocket) leaves

Serves: 4
Preparation: 5 minutes
    + 1 hour to marinate
Cooking: 15 minutes
Level: 1

■ ■ ■ *Tandoori paste is a bright red spice mixture made with garlic, ginger, cardamom, cumin, and many other spices. It is available online and wherever Indian foods are sold.*

ORANGE-GLAZED CHICKEN WITH COUSCOUS

Mix the orange juice and honey in a large bowl. • Use a sharp knife to score the chicken skin, making diagonal cuts to form a diamond pattern and making sure that you don't cut into the flesh. • Coat the chicken with the orange mixture. Cover with plastic wrap (cling film) and refrigerate for 1 hour. • Put the couscous in a medium bowl. Add the chicken stock and orange zest. • Cover the bowl with plastic wrap and let stand for 10 minutes, until the couscous has completely absorbed the liquid. • Fluff up the couscous with a fork. • Place a grill pan over medium-high heat. • Grill the chicken for 5 minutes on each side, until cooked through. • Let rest in a warm place for 5 minutes. • Slice the chicken and serve hot on a bed of the couscous.

Finely shredded zest and juice of 2 oranges

2 tablespoons honey

4 boneless chicken breasts, with skin on

$1^1/_2$ cups (300 g) instant couscous

$1^1/_2$ cups (375 ml) chicken stock, heated

Serves: 4
Preparation: 25 minutes
+ 1 hour to marinate
+ 15 minutes to stand
Cooking: 10 minutes
Level: 1

BALSAMIC CHICKEN WITH ROASTED TOMATOES

Use a sharp knife to score the chicken skin, making diagonal cuts to form a diamond pattern and making sure that you don't cut into the flesh. • Mix the balsamic vinegar and ¼ cup (60 ml) of oil in a medium bowl. • Coat the chicken with the balsamic vinegar mixture. Cover with plastic wrap (cling film) and refrigerate for 1 hour. • Preheat the oven to 350°F (180°C/gas 4). • Place the tomatoes on a baking sheet and drizzle with the remaining oil. Season with black pepper. • Roast for 10–15 minutes, until the tomatoes begin to soften. • Remove from the oven and set aside. • Place a grill pan over medium-high heat. • Grill the chicken for 5 minutes on each side, until cooked through. • Let rest in a warm place for 5 minutes. • Slice the chicken and serve hot with the roasted tomatoes.

4 boneless chicken breasts, with skin on

½ cup (125 ml) balsamic vinegar

⅓ cup (90 ml) extra-virgin olive oil

16 cherry tomatoes
Freshly ground black pepper

Serves: 4
Preparation: 10 minutes
+ 1 hour to marinate
+ 5 minutes to stand
Cooking: 20–25 minutes
Level: 1

SPICY CHICKEN WITH SOY NOODLES

Use a sharp knife to score the chicken skin, making diagonal cuts to form a diamond pattern and making sure that you don't cut into the flesh. • Coat the chicken in the five-spice powder and 2 tablespoons of the soy sauce in a medium bowl. Cover with plastic wrap (cling film) and refrigerate for 1 hour. • Cook the soba noodles in a large pot of salted boiling water for about 5 minutes, or until al dente. • Drain and rinse under cold running water. • Place the noodles in a large bowl. Mix in the cilantro and the remaining soy sauce. Set aside. • Place a grill pan over medium-high heat. • Grill the chicken for 5 minutes on each side until cooked through. • Let rest in a warm place for 5 minutes. • Slice the chicken and serve hot with the noodles.

4   boneless chicken
    breasts, with skin on
2   tablespoons Chinese
    five-spice powder
1/3 cup (90 ml)
    soy sauce
14 ounces (400 g)
    dried soba noodles
3   tablespoons fresh
    cilantro (coriander)
    leaves

Serves: 4
Preparation: 10 minutes
    + 1 hour to marinate
    + 5 minutes to stand
Cooking: 15 minutes
Level: 1

■ ■ ■ *Soba noodles are a Japanese specialty made from buckwheat flour. Find them wherever Japanese foods are sold.*

CHICKEN

LIME AND
CILANTRO CHICKEN

244

Mix 2 tablespoons of the cilantro, the sesame oil, and lime zest and juice in a large bowl. • Coat the chicken with the lime mixture. Cover with plastic wrap (cling film) and refrigerate for 1 hour. • Bring a large saucepan of salted water to a boil. • Add the rice and cook over medium heat for 10–15 minutes until tender. • Drain well and keep warm. • Place a grill pan over medium-high heat. • Grill the chicken for 5 minutes on each side, until cooked through. • Let rest in a warm place for 5 minutes. • Slice the chicken and arrange on top of the rice. • Garnish with the remaining 2 tablespoons cilantro leaves and serve hot.

4   tablespoons fresh cilantro (coriander) leaves
2   tablespoons Asian sesame oil
    Finely grated zest and juice of 4 limes
4   boneless, skinless chicken breasts
1¹/₂ cups (300 g) jasmine rice

Serves: 4
Preparation: 10 minutes
  + 1 hour to marinate
  + 5 minutes to stand
Cooking: 20–25 minutes
Level: 1

SUN-DRIED TOMATO CHICKEN WITH SPINACH

Coat the chicken with the pesto in a large bowl. Cover with plastic wrap (cling film) and refrigerate for 1 hour. • Dry-fry the pancetta in a medium saucepan over medium heat for 3 minutes until crispy. • Remove and set aside. • Pour in the cream and bring to a boil. Decrease the heat and simmer over low heat until the cream has reduced by half. • Meanwhile, place a grill pan over medium-high heat. • Grill the chicken for 5 minutes on each side until cooked through. • Let rest in a warm place for 5 minutes. • Add the spinach to the cream and cook until wilted. • Stir in the pancetta. • Serve the chicken hot with the creamy spinach.

4 boneless, skinless chicken breasts

1/3 cup (90 ml) sun-dried tomato pesto

12 slices pancetta

2 cups (500 ml) light (single) cream

6 cups (300 g) baby spinach leaves

Serves: 4
Preparation: 10 minutes
+ 1 hour to marinate
+ 5 minutes to stand
Cooking: 20 minutes
Level: 1

THYME ROASTED CHICKEN WITH NEW POTATOES

Preheat the oven to 350°F (180°C/gas 4).
• Brush the oil over and inside the cavity of the chicken and sprinkle with the thyme. Season with salt and place in a large baking dish. Cover with aluminum foil. • Bake for 1 hour. • Parboil the potatoes in boiling water for 5 minutes. Drain well and add to the baking dish with the chicken. • Bake, uncovered, for about 30 minutes, until the chicken juices run clear and the potatoes are cooked. • Serve the chicken hot with the potatoes.

$1/4$ cup (60 ml) extra-virgin olive oil

1 (3-pound/1.5-kg) chicken

5 tablespoons fresh lemon thyme leaves

1 tablespoon coarse salt

$1^1/4$ pounds (550 g) new potatoes

Serves: 4
Preparation: 10 minutes
Cooking: 1 hour 35 minutes
Level: 1

RED THAI CHICKEN

Coat the chicken with the red curry paste in a large bowl. Cover with plastic wrap (cling film) and refrigerate for 1 hour. • Preheat the oven to 425°F (220°C/gas 7). • Arrange the chicken in a single layer in a large baking dish. • Bake for about 25 minutes, or until the juices run clear. • Meanwhile, bring the stock to a boil in a medium saucepan. • Add the rice and cook over medium heat for 12 minutes. Stir in the peas and cook for 3 minutes, until the rice is tender. • Serve the chicken hot with the rice and peas.

4 chicken leg quarters

$1/4$ cup (60 ml) Thai red curry paste

2 cups (500 ml) chicken stock

$1^1/2$ cups (300 g) basmati rice

1 cup (125 g) frozen peas

Serves: 4
Preparation: 5 minutes
 + 1 hour to marinate
Cooking: 40 minutes
Level: 1

TOMATO AND TARRAGON CHICKEN

Preheat the oven to 350°F (180°C/gas 4).
• Combine the chicken, tomatoes, onions, olives, and tarragon in a large baking dish. • Bake for 30 minutes, until the chicken is cooked through. • Serve hot.

4   chicken leg quarters

$3^{1}/_{2}$ cups (875 g) peeled and chopped tomatoes, with juice

2   red onions, thinly sliced

$^{1}/_{2}$ cup (50 g) black olives

2   tablespoons fresh tarragon leaves

Serves: 4
Preparation: 5 minutes
Cooking: 30 minutes
Level: 1

CUMIN CHICKEN KEBABS

Soak twelve bamboo skewers in cold water for 30 minutes so that they don't burn. Combine the oil and cumin in a large bowl. • Coat the chicken with the cumin mixture. Cover with plastic wrap (cling film) and refrigerate for 1 hour. • Carefully thread the chicken onto the skewers and set aside. • Place a grill pan over medium-high heat. • Grill the chicken for 5 minutes on each side until cooked through. • Serve the chicken hot with the salad greens and yogurt.

3 tablespoons extra-virgin olive oil

2 tablespoons ground cumin

6 boneless, skinless chicken breasts, cut into small pieces

3 cups (150 g) mixed salad greens

1 cup (250 ml) plain yogurt

Serves: 4–6
Preparation: 40 minutes
  + 1 hour to marinate
Cooking: 10 minutes
Level: 1

PORK, LAMB, AND BEEF

BAKED PORK CUTLETS WITH ZUCCHINI

Mix the lemon juice, oil, and olives in a small bowl. • Pour the mixture over the pork in a large bowl. Cover with plastic wrap (cling film) and refrigerate for 1 hour. • Preheat the oven to 400°F (200°C/gas 6). • Place a large nonstick frying pan over medium-high heat. • Cook the pork for 2 minutes on each side, until browned. • Transfer the pork to a large baking dish and add the zucchini and the marinade. • Bake for 15–20 minutes, turning the cutlets halfway through, until the pork and zucchini are tender. • Serve hot with the lemon quarters.

3   lemons, 1 juiced and 2 cut into quarters

1/4   cup (60 ml) rosemary-infused olive oil

1/2   cup (50 g) black olives

4   bone-in pork cutlets, cut about 3/4 inch (2 cm) thick

6   zucchini (courgettes), cut in half lengthwise

Serves: 4
Preparation: 5 minutes
   + 1 hour to marinate
Cooking: 20–25 minutes
Level: 1

PORK STEAKS
WITH BAKED APPLES

Preheat the oven to 350°F (180°C/gas 4).
• Arrange the apple slices in a single
layer in a large baking dish and drizzle
with the maple syrup. • Fry the pork in
2 tablespoons of oil in a large frying pan
over medium-high heat on each side for
2 minutes, until browned. • Remove from
the pan and arrange on top of the apples.
Drizzle with the remaining 2 tablespoons
of oil. • Bake for 12–14 minutes, until the
pork is tender and the apples have
softened. • Arrange the pork on a bed of
the apples on individual serving plates.
Sprinkle with the walnuts, drizzle with
the pan juices, and serve hot.

4   apples, cored
     and sliced
     into rounds

3   tablespoons
     pure maple syrup

4   pork loin steaks,
     cut about 3/4 inch
     (2 cm) thick

1/4 cup (60 ml)
     extra-virgin olive oil

3/4 cup (120 g) walnuts,
     toasted

Serves: 4
Preparation: 10 minutes
Cooking: 16–18 minutes
Level: 1

PLUM PORK SPARERIBS

Place the spareribs in a large bowl and cover with the plum sauce. Cover with plastic wrap (cling film) and refrigerate for 1 hour. • Bring a large saucepan of salted water to a boil. • Add the rice and cook over medium heat for 10–15 minutes, until tender. • Drain well and set aside. • Place a grill pan over medium-high heat. • Brush the grill with the sesame oil. • Grill the spareribs for 5–6 minutes on each side, until cooked through. • Arrange a bed of the rice on individual serving plates and top with the spareribs. Garnish with the cilantro and serve hot.

12 pork spareribs

$2/3$ cup (150 ml) Chinese plum sauce

$1^1/2$ cups (300 g) white and wild rice mix

3 tablespoons Asian sesame oil

3 tablespoons fresh cilantro (coriander) leaves

Serves: 4–6
Preparation: 5 minutes
  + 1 hour to marinate
Cooking: 20–27 minutes
Level: 1

TERIYAKI PORK WITH ASIAN GREENS

Place the pork in a large bowl and cover with the teriyaki sauce. Cover with plastic wrap (cling film) and refrigerate for 1 hour. • Preheat the oven to 375°F (190°C/gas 5). • Place a large nonstick frying pan over medium-high heat. • Cook the pork for 2 minutes on each side until browned. • Transfer the pork to a large baking dish. • Bake for 15–20 minutes until tender. • Remove from the oven and let rest for 5 minutes. • Cook the choy sum in a large saucepan of boiling water for 1 minute. • Add the bok choy and cook for 1–2 minutes, until both vegetables are tender. • Drain well and return to the pan. Add the sesame seeds and toss well. • Slice the pork thickly and serve hot with the Asian greens.

3 pork tenderloins (fillets) (about 12 ounces/350 g each)

3/4 cup (180 ml) teriyaki sauce

1 bunch choy sum, trimmed

2 bunches baby bok choy, cut in half lengthwise

3 tablespoons sesame seeds

Serves: 4–6
Preparation: 10 minutes
+ 1 hour to chill
+ 5 minutes to rest
Cooking: 15–18 minutes
Level: 1

SPICED PORK WITH CABBAGE

Sprinkle the pork with the five-spice powder. • Fry the pork in 3 tablespoons of the oil in a large frying pan over medium-high heat for 5–6 minutes on each side, until tender and cooked to your liking. • Remove from the pan and let rest while you prepare the vegetables. • Heat the remaining 1 tablespoon of oil in a medium saucepan over low heat. • Add the onion and cook for 3 minutes. • Add the cabbage and cook for 4 minutes until wilted. • Slice the pork thickly and serve hot on a bed of the cabbage.

3   pork tenderloins (fillets) (about 12 ounces/350 g each)
2   tablespoons five-spice powder
1/4 cup (60 ml) Asian sesame oil
1   onion, thinly sliced
1/2 Savoy cabbage, cored and finely shredded

Serves: 4–6
Preparation: 10 minutes
Cooking: 15 minutes
Level: 1

LAMB CUTLETS
WITH MINTED PEAS

Preheat the oven to 375°F (190°C/gas 5).
• Fry the lamb in the oil from the
marinated feta in a large frying pan over
medium-high heat for 2 minutes on each
side, until browned. • Transfer the lamb
to a large baking dish. • Bake for 5–10
minutes, until tender. • Remove from the
oven and let rest for 5 minutes. • Cook
the peas in a small saucepan of boiling
water for 1 minute, until cooked. • Mix
the peas, feta, mint, and raspberry
vinegar in a medium bowl and toss well.
• Serve the lamb hot with the pea and
feta salad.

8   lamb cutlets,
    trimmed
5   ounces (150 g)
    marinated feta, oil
    reserved, cut into
    small cubes
1½ cups (185 g)
    frozen peas, thawed
3   tablespoons leaves
    fresh mint
3   tablespoons
    raspberry vinegar

Serves: 6–8
Preparation: 5 minutes
    + 5 minutes to rest
Cooking: 10–15 minutes
Level: 1

PESTO LAMB WITH NEW POTATOES

Place the lamb in a large bowl and cover with the pesto. Cover with plastic wrap (cling film) and chill for 1 hour. • Cook the potatoes in a large pot of boiling water for 15–20 minutes until tender. • Drain well and return to the pan. Add the butter and chives and toss well. • Cook the lamb in a nonstick frying pan over medium-high heat for 3–4 minutes on each side, until cooked through, but still slightly pink. • Slice the lamb thickly and serve hot with the potatoes.

4　lamb tenderloins (fillets), weighing about 6 ounces (180 g) each

$1/2$　cup (125 ml) store-bought basil pesto

$1^1/4$　pounds (550 g) new potatoes

3　tablespoons butter, cut up

2　tablespoons chopped chives

Serves: 4
Preparation: 10 minutes + 1 hour to chill
Cooking: 18–24 minutes
Level: 1

COCONUT LAMB WITH RICE

Cook the lamb with the tomatoes in a large frying pan over medium heat for 2 minutes. • Pour in the coconut milk. • Cover and cook over low heat for 35–40 minutes until the lamb is tender. • Meanwhile, bring a large saucepan of salted water to a boil. • Add the rice and cook over medium heat for 10–15 minutes, until tender. • Drain well and set aside. • Add the cilantro to the lamb. • Serve hot on a bed of the rice.

1³/₄ pounds (800 g) lamb fillet (tenderloin), diced

6   tomatoes, coarsely chopped

2   cups (500 ml) coconut milk

1¹/₂ cups (300 g) basmati rice

3   tablespoons fresh cilantro (coriander) leaves

Serves: 4
Preparation: 10 minutes
Cooking: 47–57 minutes
Level: 1

LAMB KLEFTIKO

Preheat the oven to 300°F (150°C/gas 2). • Put all the ingredients in a large baking dish. Cover with aluminum foil. • Bake for about 2 hours, until the lamb is tender. • Remove from the oven. Pour the liquid into a small saucepan. • Bring to a boil over high heat and cook until reduced by half. • Arrange the lamb and shallots in individual serving bowls. • Pour the cooking liquid into the bowls and serve hot.

8 lamb chops, cut about $1/2$ inch (1.5 cm) thick

12 shallots, unpeeled

2 cups (500 ml) dry white wine

Finely shredded zest and juice of 2 lemons

3 tablespoons fresh oregano leaves

Serves: 4
Preparation: 10 minutes
Cooking: 2 hours
Level: 1

■ ■ ■ *In this classic Greek dish, the lamb is sealed in a baking dish and slowly baked until tender and succulent. There are many legends surrounding its invention. According to some, the Greeks learned to make it when they were fighting to free themselves from Ottoman rule. Hidden in the mountains, Greek soldiers would place all the ingredients in a dish and bury it over hot embers in the ground. No enticing food smells would emerge to let the enemy know their position.*

LAMB KOFTE WITH MINTED COUSCOUS

Combine the lamb and bell pepper in a food processor and process until a coarse paste forms. • Use wet hands to shape the mixture into twelve sausage-shaped lengths. • Thread each kofte onto a metal skewer. • Mix the couscous and mint in a medium bowl. • Pour the stock over the couscous mixture. • Cover the bowl with plastic wrap (cling film) and let stand for 10 minutes, until the couscous has completely absorbed the liquid. • Fluff up the couscous with a fork and set aside. • Place a grill pan over high heat. • Grill the kofte for about 5 minutes on each side, until cooked through. • Serve hot on a bed of the minted couscous.

$1^1/2$ pounds (750 g) ground (minced) lamb

1   red bell pepper (capsicum), seeded and finely chopped

2   cups (400 g) instant couscous

3   tablespoons finely chopped fresh mint

2   cups (500 ml) chicken stock, hot

Serves: 4
Preparation: 15 minutes
   + 10 minutes to stand
Cooking: 10 minutes
Level: 1

FIVE-SPICE STEAK WITH WILTED SPINACH

Heat the oil in a large frying pan over medium-high heat. • Sprinkle the steaks with the five-spice powder. • Cook for 3–4 minutes on each side, depending on how well done you like your steak. • Remove from the heat. Cover and let rest for 5 minutes. • Cook the spinach in a medium saucepan of boiling water for 30 seconds until wilted. • Drain and return to the pan. Add the soy sauce and toss well. • Serve the steaks hot with the spinach.

3   tablespoons Asian
    sesame oil

4   thick beef
    fillet steaks, about 6
    ounces (180 g) each

2   tablespoons
    five-spice powder

10 ounces (300 g)
    baby spinach leaves

1/4 cup (60 ml)
    soy sauce

Serves: 4
Preparation: 5 minutes
Cooking: 8 minutes
    + 5 minutes to rest
Level: 1

BEEF RIB ROAST WITH CRISPY POTATOES

Preheat the oven to 400°F (200°C/ gas 6). • Sear the beef in $1/4$ cup (60 ml) oil in a large frying pan over high heat for 2 minutes on each side until browned all over. • Transfer to a large roasting pan and season with salt and peppercorns. • Roast for about 25–35 minutes, depending on how well done you like your beef. • Remove from the oven and let rest for 10 minutes. • Meanwhile, cook the potatoes in a large pot of boiling water for 5 minutes. • Drain and toss to smash them slightly. • Pour the remaining $1/2$ cup (125 ml) oil in a large roasting pan and heat in the oven for 10 minutes. • Add the potatoes and roast for about 30 minutes, until crispy. • Slice the rib roast into portions and serve hot with the potatoes.

3   pounds (1.5 kg) standing rib roast (rib of beef), trimmed

$3/4$ cup (180 ml) extra-virgin olive oil

Salt

4   tablespoons green peppercorns

$1^1/4$ pounds (550 g) new potatoes, cut in half

Serves: 4
Preparation: 20 minutes
  + 10 minutes to rest
Cooking: 35–40 minutes
Level: 1

BALSAMIC STEAK WITH CARAMELIZED ONIONS

Cook the onions in 2 tablespoons of the oil in a large frying pan over very low heat for about 30 minutes, or until caramelized. • Meanwhile, heat the balsamic vinegar in a small saucepan over medium heat until it reduces by half. • Heat the remaining 2 tablespoons oil in a large frying pan over medium-high heat. • Cook the steaks for 3–4 minutes on each side, depending on how well done you like your steak. • Remove from the heat. Cover and let rest for 5 minutes. • Place the steaks on individual serving plates, topped with the onions and balsamic sauce with the arugula on the side.

6 onions, thinly sliced

1/4 cup (60 ml) extra-virgin olive oil

3/4 cup (180 ml) balsamic vinegar

4 thick beef fillet steaks, about 6 ounces (180 g) each

2 cups (100 g) arugula (rocket) leaves

Serves: 4
Preparation: 10 minutes + 5 minutes
Cooking: 40 minutes
Level: 1

SMOKY STEAK WITH TOMATO SALAD

Put the beef in a large bowl and cover with the marinade. Cover with plastic wrap (cling film) and refrigerate for 1 hour. • Place a grill pan over medium-high heat. • Cook the steaks for 4–5 minutes each, depending on how well done you like your steak. • Remove from the heat. Cover and let rest for 5 minutes. • Serve the steak hot, topped with the tomatoes, onion, and olives.

4   fillet beef steaks, about 6 ounces (180 g) each, cut about 3/4 inch (2 cm) thick

3/4 cup (180 ml) smoky barbecue sauce

6   tomatoes, thinly sliced

1   red onion, thinly sliced

1/2 cup (50 g) black olives, pitted

Serves: 4
Preparation: 10 minutes
   + 1 hour to chill
   + 5 minutes to stand
Cooking: 8–10 minutes
Level: 1

BEEF STROGANOFF

286

Bring a large saucepan of salted water to a boil. • Add the rice and cook over medium heat for 10–15 minutes, until tender. • Drain well and set aside. • Cook the beef and mushrooms in a large nonstick frying pan over medium-high heat for 3 minutes. • Stir in the sour cream and thyme. • Decrease the heat to low and simmer for about 7 minutes, or until the beef and mushrooms are tender. • Serve the stroganoff hot with the rice and garnished with the extra sprigs of thyme.

1½ cups (300 g) basmati rice

1 pound (500 g) beef fillet, cut into thin strips

1 pound (500 g) mushrooms, thinly sliced

1¼ cups (310 ml) sour cream

3 tablespoons finely chopped fresh thyme + sprigs to garnish

Serves: 4
Preparation: 10 minutes
Cooking: 20–25 minutes
Level: 1

DESSERTS

GRILLED PEACHES WITH MINT YOGURT

Mix the yogurt and mint in a small bowl and refrigerate. • Dip the peach halves in the orange juice and sprinkle with the brown sugar. • Place a grill pan over medium-high heat. • Grill the peaches for 4 minutes on each side. • Serve the peaches warm with the mint yogurt.

3/4 cup (180 ml) plain yogurt

2 tablespoons fresh mint leaves

4 peaches, cut in half and pitted

2 tablespoons freshly squeezed orange juice

1/4 cup (50 g) firmly packed dark brown sugar

Serves: 4
Preparation: 10 minutes
Cooking: 8 minutes
Level: 1

GINGER POACHED PEARS

Combine the pears, water, superfine sugar, orange zest and juice, and ginger in a large saucepan. • Simmer over low heat for 30 minutes until the pears have just softened. • Remove the pears from the liquid and set aside. • Turn up the heat and boil for 10 minutes. • Return the pears to the liquid. • Serve warm.

8   small pears, peeled

4   cups (1 liter) water

1   cup (200 g) superfine (caster) sugar

   Juice and finely grated zest of 2 oranges

3   tablespoons candied or preserved ginger, finely sliced

Serves: 4
Preparation: 10 minutes
Cooking: 40 minutes
Level: 1

BAKED APPLES WITH MAPLE SYRUP

Preheat the oven to 350°F (180°C/gas 4).
• Core the apples and lightly score the skin around the edge with a sharp knife.
• Mix the dates and walnuts in a small bowl. • Stuff the mixture into the apples.
• Arrange the apples in a baking pan.
• Mix the maple syrup and water in a small bowl and pour over the apples.
• Bake for about 50 minutes, or until the apples have softened. • Serve warm.

4   large apples
6   pitted dates,
    finely chopped
1/2 cup (50 g) finely
    chopped walnuts
1/2 cup (125 ml)
    pure maple syrup
1/2 cup (125 ml) water

Serves: 4
Preparation: 10 minutes
Cooking: 50 minutes
Level: 1

GOOEY CHOCOLATE PUDDING

Preheat the oven to 400°F (200°C/ gas 6). • Grease four small ramekins with 1 tablespoon of the butter and sprinkle with the superfine sugar, shaking out the excess. • Melt the chocolate and remaining 7 tablespoons butter in a double boiler over barely simmering water. • Set aside. • Beat the eggs, egg yolks, and remaining superfine sugar in a large bowl with an electric mixer at high speed until pale and thick. • Use a large rubber spatula to fold the chocolate mixture and flour into the beaten eggs. • Pour the mixture evenly into the prepared ramekins. • Bake for about 10 minutes, or until set. • Serve warm.

$1/2$ cup (125 g) butter, cut up

$1/2$ cup (100 g) superfine (caster) sugar

4 ounces (125 g) semisweet or dark chocolate, coarsely chopped

2 large eggs and 2 large egg yolks

2 teaspoons all-purpose (plain) flour

Serves: 4
Preparation: 15 minutes
Cooking: 10 minutes
Level: 1

STRAWBERRY FROZEN YOGURT

298

Process the strawberries, confectioners' sugar, and lemon juice in a food processor until smooth. • Transfer the mixture into a large bowl. • Stir in the yogurt and whipped cream until well mixed. • If you have an ice-cream machine, pour the mixture into it and follow the instructions. • If you don't have an ice-cream machine, freeze the mixture for 9 hours, stirring well every 3 hours. • Scoop into bowls to serve.

1 cup (250 g) strawberries, hulled

2/3 cup (100 g) confectioners' (icing) sugar

1/3 cup (90 ml) freshly squeezed lemon juice

1 cup (250 ml) plain yogurt

2/3 cup (150 ml) whipped cream

Serves: 4
Preparation: 15 minutes
+ time to freeze
Level: 1

CHOCOLATE MINT SORBET

Bring the water and superfine sugar to a boil in a medium saucepan. • Decrease the heat to low and simmer until the sugar has dissolved. • Stir in the cocoa powder and mint. Simmer for 15 minutes. • Remove from the heat and let cool completely. • If you have an ice-cream machine, pour the mixture into it and follow the instructions. • If you don't have an ice-cream machine, freeze the mixture for 9 hours, stirring well every 3 hours. • Scoop into bowls and serve with the wafers.

$2^3/_4$ cups (680 ml) water

1 cup (200 g) superfine (caster) sugar

1 cup (150 g) unsweetened cocoa powder

4 sprigs fresh mint, finely chopped

Ice cream wafers or other thin, crisp cookies, to serve

Serves: 4
Preparation: 20 minutes + time to freeze
Cooking: 20 minutes
Level: 1

ESPRESSO GRANITA

Combine the superfine sugar and cocoa powder in a large saucepan. Slowly mix in the water until smooth. • Bring to a boil, stirring often, until the sugar has dissolved. • Decrease the heat to low and simmer for 3 minutes. • Remove from the heat and stir in the coffee. • Pour the mixture into a freezeproof container and let cool completely. • Freeze for 2 hours until partly set. • Remove and stir with a fork to break up the ice crystals. • Return to the freezer and freeze for 2 hours.
• Stir again to break up the ice crystals.
• Serve in espresso cups, with the whipped cream on the side if liked.

1   cup (200 g) superfine (caster) sugar
1 1/2 tablespoons unsweetened cocoa powder
1/2 cup (125 ml) water
5   cups (1.25 liters) very strong brewed coffee
1   cup (250 ml) whipped cream (optional)

Serves: 4
Preparation: 20 minutes + 4 hours to freeze
Cooking: 5 minutes
Level: 1

VANILLA PANNA COTTA

Mix the cream, superfine sugar, and vanilla seeds in a medium saucepan.
• Bring to a boil and simmer over low heat for 2 minutes. • Remove from the heat. • Stir in the gelatin mixture until completely dissolved. • Spoon the mixture evenly into four 7-ounce (200-g) custard cups, ramekins, or dariole molds.
• Chill for 6 hours, until set. • Turn the panna cotta out onto serving plates.
• Serve with fresh strawberries.

2 cups (500 ml) light (single) cream

1/2 cup (100 g) superfine (caster) sugar

Seeds of 1 vanilla pod

2 teaspoons plain gelatin, soaked in 2 tablespoons cold water until softened

1 cup (250 g) strawberries, hulled

Serves: 4
Preparation: 15 minutes + 6 hours to chill
Cooking: 5 minutes
Level: 1

CHOCOLATE AND RASPBERRY TART

Preheat the oven to 350°F (180°C/gas 4).
• Line a 10-inch (25-cm) tart pan with a
removable bottom with the pastry. • Prick
all over with a fork. • Bake for 15
minutes. • Reduce the oven temperature
to 300°F (150°C/gas 2). • Melt the
chocolate with the cream in a double
boiler over barely simmering water.
• Transfer to a large bowl. • With an
electric mixer at high speed, beat in the
egg yolks. • Use a large rubber spatula to
fold in the raspberries. • Pour the
mixture into pastry shell. • Bake for
25–30 minutes, until the filling has set.
• Let cool completely and serve.

1	sheet shortcrust pie pastry
10	ounces (300 g) semisweet or dark chocolate
2	cups (500 ml) light (single) cream
4	large egg yolks
1	cup (250 g) fresh raspberries

Serves: 6–8
Preparation: 10 minutes
Cooking: 40–45 minutes
Level: 1

PORTUGUESE-STYLE CRÈME CARAMEL

Preheat the oven to 350°F (180°C/gas 4).
• Combine the brown sugar and water in a small saucepan. Stir over low heat until the sugar dissolves. • Turn up the heat to medium and bring to a boil. • Cook for about 6 minutes, or until the syrup thickens. • Pour the syrup into an 8-inch (20-cm) round springform pan. • With an electric mixer at high speed, beat the eggs and egg yolks and superfine sugar in a large bowl until pale and creamy. • Bring the milk to a boil in a medium saucepan. • Gradually whisk the hot milk into the egg mixture. • Pour the mixture into the springform pan. • Place in a large roasting pan. Pour boiling water into the roasting pan to come halfway up the sides of the springform pan. • Bake for about 1 hour, or until the custard has set. • Let the custard cool completely in the waterbath. • Chill overnight. • Gently run a knife around the edge of the custard. Turn out onto a plate and serve.

$^{1}/_{2}$ cup (100 g) firmly packed dark brown sugar

1 tablespoon water

6 large eggs and 6 large egg yolks

$2^{1}/_{3}$ cups (470 g) superfine (caster) sugar

$3^{2}/_{3}$ cups (900 ml) milk

Serves: 6
Preparation: 10 minutes
  + overnight to chill
Cooking: 70 minutes
Level: 2

BLUEBERRY MERINGUES

Preheat the oven to 300°F (150°C/gas 2). • Line two baking sheets with parchment (baking) paper and mark four 3-inch (8-cm) circles on the paper. • Beat the egg whites in a large bowl with an electric mixer at medium speed until frothy. • With mixer at high speed, gradually add the superfine sugar, beating until stiff, glossy peaks form. • Spread the mixture into rounds on the prepared sheets. • Bake for 40–45 minutes until crisp. • Turn off the oven and leave the door ajar until the meringues are completely cool. • Carefully remove the paper. • Mix the blueberries and hazelnut liqueur in a small bowl. • Stir in the cream. • Sandwich the meringues together in pairs with the blueberry liqueur cream and serve immediately.

4   **large egg whites**

1   **cup (250 g) superfine (caster) sugar**

1¹/₂ **cups (375 g) blueberries**

2   **tablespoons hazelnut liqueur**

2   **cups (500 ml) whipped cream**

Serves: 4
Preparation: 25 minutes
  + cooling time
Cooking: 40–45 minutes
Level: 1

APPLE TURNOVERS

Preheat the oven to 400°F (200°C/ gas 6). • Cut the pastry into four squares. • Place an apple quarter in the center of each pastry square. • Draw up the pastry edges and pinch them together to seal. • Arrange the turnovers on a baking sheet. • Bake for 15–20 minutes until golden. • Mix the water and corn syrup and drizzle over the turnovers. • Serve hot with a scoop of ice cream.

1	sheet puff pastry
1	apple, peeled, cored, and cut into quarters
1/2	cup (125 ml) hot water
1/4	cup (60 ml) light corn syrup or golden syrup
4	scoops good-quality vanilla ice cream

Serves: 4
Preparation: 10 minutes
Cooking: 15–20 minutes
Level: 1

BRANDY SNAPS

Preheat the oven to 325°F (170°C/gas 3). • Line two cookie sheets with parchment (baking) paper. • Butter two rolling pins. • Melt the butter with the brown sugar and corn syrup in a small saucepan over low heat, stirring constantly until the sugar has dissolved. • Remove from the heat and let cool completely. • Mix in the flour. Drop teaspoons of the mixture 2 inches (5 cm) apart onto the prepared sheets. • Bake for 8–10 minutes until golden brown. • Working quickly, use a spatula to lift each cookie from the sheet and drape it over a rolling pin. • Slide each cookie off the pin onto a rack to finish cooling. • If the cookies harden too quickly, return the cookie sheets to the oven for 1–2 minutes, or until the cookies are soft again. • Beat the cream in a medium bowl until stiff. • Spoon the cream into a pastry bag fitted with a small plain tip. • Fill the brandy snaps with the cream and serve immediately.

$1/2$ cup (125 g) butter, cut up

1 cup (200 g) firmly packed dark brown sugar

$1/2$ cup (125 ml) light corn syrup or golden syrup

$3/4$ cup (125 g) all-purpose (plain) flour

2 cups (500 ml) heavy (double) cream

Serves: 4–6
Preparation: 25 minutes
Cooking: 8–10 minutes
    per batch
Level: 1

INDEX